John Wycliffe

Morning Star of the Reformation

D1593921

John Wycliffe

Morning Star of the Reformation

Edwin Robertson

marshalls

Marshalls Paperbacks
Marshall Morgan & Scott
3 Beggarwood Lane, Basingstoke,
Hants, RG23 7LP, UK

First published by Marshall Morgan & Scott Ltd 1984

ISBN   0 551 01142 4

Typeset by PRG TypoGraphics, Cheddar, Somerset
Printed in Great Britain by Anchor Brendon Limited,
Tiptree, Essex

Contents

Introduction

During an interview with Michael Charlton on Channel 4, Tony Benn said in a casual aside, 'I am not a Marxist'. That must have suprised many opponents and supporters of the radical Labour politician. Yet he had earlier established in a sermon preached in St James's, Piccadilly, that his radical roots went back, not to Marx but to fourteenth century England. Radical politicians in England do not have to learn from Karl Marx or Soviet Russia. They can go back before the Russian Revolution of 1917, before the French Revolution of 1789, to England's own revolution in 1649 and even further to the Peasants' Revolt of 1381.

Something similar is true of Protestant church people. During the 500th anniversary celebrations of the birth of Martin Luther, English Protestants honoured the great Reformer, but were also aware that he was not the source of their Protestantism. Like Tony Benn, they too could go back to the fourteenth century, when most of the ideas later championed by Martin Luther in Germany were already being preached by John Wycliffe and the Lollards. In fact, most English Protestants and all Free Church people, including their American counterparts, are much happier with Wycliffe than with Luther, who basically remained a Catholic to the end of his days and could break away neither from the Catholic view of the Mass nor the Roman attitude to church and state.

Both politician and Protestant go back to the same period for the beginning of their reforming ideas and both find their sources in one man: John Wycliffe. Wycliffe was born in Yorkshire about 1324, studied in the University of Oxford where he spent most of his life, and become rector of Lutterworth, where he lived for the last two or three years of his life after his expulsion from Oxford. From that Leicestershire village, there arose a religious movement which inspired a Reformation in church and state. The Establishment may have had to wait until the time of Henry VIII for their Reformation, but the people had theirs in the Lollard movement, whose poor preachers proclaimed the authority of the Bible above that of the church and asserted the right of private judgement in matters of church and state.

The Lollards were half inside and half outside the church. They attacked the wealth of the church and sought to relieve the poverty of their day by disendowment, and they renewed the spiritual life of the church by a return to a study of the Bible. John Wycliffe, who died in December 1384, was their mentor and inspiration. The time was not then ripe for new structures, such as would be necessary later in the days of Luther, Calvin and Cranmer, for success was not even distantly in sight.

In England, every effort was made to eradicate all trace of Wycliffe's teaching and to vilify his person. Even his body was dug up and burned, so that his ashes might be shaken into the river. There is no record of him left, except strings of abusive epithets from his enemies. His writings were all destroyed in England. Fortunately, the Hussites of Bohemia preserved them.

This short study of one who has been aptly called 'the morning star of the Reformation' attempts to show the impact of Wycliffe's mind upon his generation and the continuing effect upon the religious and political ideas of this country. It can portray little of his personality, for little is known. It will not attempt to study his writings chronologically or in detail, because the chronology is uncertain and the writings are of a very medieval character. Wycliffe was a child of the Middle Ages and could only have his ideas taken seriously by using the pedantic arguments familiar to the scholastic philosophers of his time. This style makes his Latin books obscure to modern readers. A study of his English pamphlets will be attempted but even these, although in the simple and vigorous language of the day, have, to quote

GM Trevelyan, 'a certain want of attractiveness, owing to the predominance of hard intellectual and moral qualities over the emotions'. His writings tell us little about himself except his severity, which we can assume to be characteristic for it also emerges in his actions.

We can only understand this severe Oxford scholar who rocked the Middle Ages if we make the attempt to put our minds back into the fourteenth century, the time of Chaucer and William Langland, the rumbustious world of the *Canterbury Tales* and the gloomy piety of *Piers Plowman*. This land of England, which had known the glorious triumphs of the early years of Edward III's reign, when one third of France was under its domination, was in decline by Wycliffe's day. The total dominance of the church was replaced by the corruption of John of Gaunt and Henry Percy; the oppression of the aristocracy was challenged effectively by the Good Parliament, only to be dissolved by weak kings. At last the people rose in the Peasants' Revolt of 1381. Although they understood neither his Latin nor his tortuous logic, the people saw in Wycliffe one who opened up the Bible to them, a champion of their cause. Yet he never approved of their violence.

But we must do more than look back to the fourteenth century if we are to realise how important is this 600th anniversary of the death of Wycliffe for us today. We must show what lights he lit to guide England through the dark days ahead: the Wars of the Roses, the English Reformation, the Civil War, the growth of democracy, the Industrial Revolution, the rediscovery of the authority of the Bible, the growth of Nonconformity and the Evangelical Movement. Of course, other streams flowed into the course of English history, but for Evangelical reform and political democracy, Wycliffe was the most significant stream.

In order to establish these large claims for Wycliffe, it will be necessary to look at his ideas, not only in the light of his day, but in the ongoing history of this country. The ideas will inevitably fall into two parts: the religious, which includes his attacks upon medieval doctrines as well as his translation of the Bible; and the political, which includes his pleas for a decent standard of living and a redistribution of wealth, also based upon the Bible. His religious ideas became part of the history of Christianity in England largely through his assertion of the authority of the Bible, and his passion to make it available in a language which all could understand. His political ideas, which cover church and state, were hindered for a while by the failure of the Peasants' Revolt, but smouldered underground to blaze forth again among the Diggers and the Levellers in Cromwell's England. The battle for the universal franchise and the cause of the suffragettes could both look to Wycliffe for inspiration. It is because of him that so many of the trade unions of England and Wales were born in chapels. It was because of him that the Labour Party, unlike its continental equivalents, has its origins in the Bible, rather than in Karl Marx.

1. The Land of Chaucer and Piers Plowman

John Wycliffe was a Yorkshireman of the fourteenth century, born in its twenties and dying on 31 December 1384. His life spanned the worst period of the Black Death, when more than a third of the population perished, and his closing years saw the terrifying Peasants' Revolt of 1381.

When the century opened, the feudal system established under William the Conqueror was still in working order, although in the process of decay. This was usually called the 'manorial' system and was based upon serfdom. The lord of the manor kept part of his cultivated land to be worked by his bailiff for his own food supply, and the rest was cultivated in small patches by the peasants or 'villeins' of the village. These men held their fields on a tenure and were not subject to eviction. But their tenure, though safe, was heavily burdened. They were not freemen of the land but they were bound to the soil. And they had many dues to pay to the lord, as well as service for so many days in the year on his 'demesne' or estate. It was on these fixed services that the lord relied for the cultivation of his land. On those days that were not claimed by the bailiff, the peasant could work on his own patch of land, from which he had to support his family and pay money rents to the lord.

The system worked reasonably well for centuries, because it gave both lord and peasants certain rights. The rights may seem limited on the peasants' side, but at least the lord could call upon his free labour only for a fixed number of days, not at all hours and for any purpose. The villein was not a slave.

The breakdown of the manorial system

Already in the previous century some peasants had done well enough on their patch of ground to enable them to buy their freedom; others had escaped into outlawry in the forests that separated the cultivated lands. The bailiff also found very often that the system provided him with poor labourers and bad farming. The villein used to use his own oxen and instruments for ploughing and these were unsuitable for the bigger lands of the lord. He often worked badly because there was no incentive for him. Fixed hours of service were frequently commuted into money rents so that the bailiff could hire and fire better workmen. At the same time, some peasants had begun to grasp the idea of complete personal freedom and felt it degrading to perform forced labour. They considered freedom to be their right. Such ideas were not general, but they were sufficiently widespread to undermine the system.

When the Black Death made labour scarce the peasants were astute enough to recognise their worth and both king and Parliament tried in vain to control their demands for higher wages.

GM Trevelyan describes this change in its early stages.

'Before the fourteenth century opened, the bailiffs had been forced to hire shepherds for the sheep, and wards for the pigs and cattle. The bond-slave, who at the time of the Conquest had driven the swine to their pannage in the acorn forests, had, partly from the influence of Christian ideas on their masters, partly from their own intense desire to be free from the collar of abject slavery, been emancipated within about a hundred years of Hastings. But it was difficult to use the villein in place of Gurth the swineherd, who had been forced to guard his master's property all the year round; for the villein owed services only on certain days of the week and the year, and during the days that were his own the lord's animals would be unguarded. So, first, the offices of herdsmen became regularly filled by hired labour. As time went on, the bailiffs began more and more to find that it was advantageous to have the ploughing done in the same way.'

The English character

The pace of this change was undoubtedly affected by the charcter of the people whom the Normans had sought to put under bondage. There is a fascinating description of this wilful character of the English by a contemporary of Wycliffe: John Trevisa, a Cornish clerk and scholar educated at Oxford. Trevisa, like many other medieval commentators, detects a paradox in the English character: the aggressiveness of Englishmen led to exceptional success in military adventure abroad at the price of extreme social and political instability at home.

'Men of the south are easier and more mild; and men of the north are more unstable, more cruel and more restless; the middle men are a mixture of the two.
The English are taken as an example of 'men of the north' . . . they go into diverse lands if they find any man richer or more fortunate than themselves in far and strange lands. They know better how to win and keep the lands of others than to look after their own inheritance. The men are able to do all kinds of deeds, but they do them quickly and hastily and also quickly leave off what they have begun. For this reason, Pope Eugenius said that the English were able to do whatever they wanted

and to be well ahead of all other men, if inconstancy did not prevent them. And as Hannibal said of the Romans, they cannot be conquered except in their own country; so the English cannot be overcome in foreign lands, but in their own country they are easily overcome. These men despise their own and prize other men's. They are never content with their own estate. It is what other men have that they would gladly take for themselves. Thus it is that yeoman arrays himself like a squire, a squire like a knight, a knight like a duke and a duke like a king'[2]

The jaundiced eye of a Cornishman perhaps, but the English certainly appeared to be arrogant and quarrelsome people. A more kindly commentator might have said 'independent'!

Such a people would find Wycliffe's thesis that lordship is based on grace a powerful idea. In John Trevisa's sense Wycliffe is very English in his argument in *De civile dominio*. There he claims that all possessions and all power, civil and ecclesiastical, are held righteously only as long as their possessor remains in grace. With ruthless logic he proceeds to the conclusion that 'a pauper, if he be in grace, has a better right to 'lordship' than a pope or an emperor in a state of mortal sin'.

John Wycliffe was more concerned with applying that argument to the wealth of the clergy, but there were others ready to apply these revolutionary ideas to the state as well as to the church.

Geoffrey Chaucer

In his Canterbury Tales, Chaucer makes us aware of the rich tapestry of English life and his characters are those who peopled Wycliffe's England. The ploughman is not absent from this varied company. After describing the poor Parson, and losing no opportunity to contrast this 'holy minded man' with the common run of clerics, Chaucer brings the plowman upon the scene and 'with him there, his brother'.

He was an honest worker, good and true.

The Plowman, like the poor Parson, is described as a Christian:

Loving God best with all his heart and mind
And then his neighbour as himself, repined
At no misfortune, slacked for no content,
For steadily about his work he went

There is nothing here of discontent, and even the oppressive taxes are paid without complaint.

Chaucer's model had been that of Boccaccio's *Decameron,* which is a collection stories supposedly told while Italy was being ravished with plague. The story-tellers are shut up in a castle and tell their stories to while away the time and to forget the awful scenes outside. Chaucer comes much nearer to the life of England and many of his stories give a true reflection of the colourful life of the fourteenth century. But he too is an escapist. There is no aspect of politics or society in those days that is truly reflected in the boisterous fun of these happy tales.

Piers Plowman

But there was another ploughman. William Langland, a poet from the Malvern Hills, brought out his first edition of *Piers Plowman* in 1362 and spent the rest of his life revising it. Trevelyen has compared the success of this book to that of Bunyan's *Pilgrim's Progress* about the time of the Civil War. It is unique in its imagery and ideas. At first it seems remote from the real world. The shepherd wanders throughout the summer season and at last dreams — marvellously:

> *All the worlds weal, all the world's woe,*
> *Truth and trickery, treason and guile,*
> *All I saw sleeping.*

Very soon the world of John Wycliffe opens up much more clearly than in Chaucer's tales of Canterbury.

> *Rich and poor, all manner of men,*
> *Working and wandering, as in the world we must.*
> *Some were for ploughing and played full seldom,*
> *Set their seed and sowed their seed, and sweated hard,*
> *To win what wastrels with gluttony destroy.*

The 'Vision of the Field Full of Folk' with which the book opens is a powerful description of the world in which William Langland lived, with all its poverty and injustice. And as he revised, his keen eye noted the twists and turns of corrupt politics, of wanton clergy and of self-seeking prelates. In one of his revisions around 1377 he added a fable comparing the Commons to an assembly of mice and rats who are consulting how to bell the cat — the old King Edward III in his senility. But he warns the Commons that even worse times will come when the old cat dies, and the kitten, the boy King Richard II succeeds. For there will then be no-one to keep order, and the horrors of anarchy will be let loose on the land.

This was a time of serious distress among the poor. Many were seeking the disendowment of the church. Wycliffe had the people with him in this proposal. The church had become the richest landowner in the country as frightened lords had given over their lands to save their souls. If the church had been disendowed, it would have been as it was when Henry VIII sacked the monastries. The wealth of the church would have gone to the lords, because it was they who had suffered through their inheritance being given away. Even Wycliffe could see no other way. He urged, however, that the newly recovered wealth should be used for the relief of the taxes which oppressed the poor. Even Piers Plowman cried, 'Take their lands, ye lords'.

While the secular lords used the persuasive power of Wycliffe to try to acquire the church lands for themselves, the people suffered. There are few better descriptions of that poverty than in *Piers Plowman:*

> *The neediest are our neighbours if we give*
> *   heed to them,*
> *Prisoners in the dungeon, the poor in the cottage,*
> *Charged with a crew of children and with*
> *   a landlords rent.*
> *What they win by their spinning to make*
> *   their porridge with,*
> *Milk and meal, to satisfy the babes, —*
> *The babes that continually cry for food —*
> *This they must spend on the rent of their houses,*
> *Ay and themselves suffer with hunger,*
> *With woe in winter rising a-nights,*
> *In the narrow room to rock the cradle,*
> *Carding, combing, clouting, washing, rubbing,*
> *   winding peeling, rushes.*
> *Pitiful is it to read the cottage women's woe.*

The horror of the Black Death was the prelude to such dire poverty that, instead of putting up wages because of shortage of labour, prices rose and wages were pegged, rents were heavier and food scarcer. The nation — or at least part of it — starved. That part became conscious of its desperate plight and eventually rose in revolt.

Religion

The role of the church in fourteenth century England was, of course, very much more pervasive than in modern times. Everyone was subject to the laws of the church, in just the same way as they were to the laws of the state. A person could become as much of an outlaw by disobedience to the one as by refusing to abide by the laws of the other. Until the second half of the fourteenth century this was hardly questioned. The standards of morality enforced by the church were acceptable to the conscience of the nation. Neither was there any serious questioning of the teaching of the church. Heresy was almost unknown in England.

Through the influence of Wycliffe, the second part of the century was very different. Two movements arose which tended in the same direction. The first was a sustained attack upon the temporal and political power of the clergy. In this, Wycliffe had the strong support of John of Gaunt, the most influential lord of that age, and while that support might occasionally have saved him, it became an encumberance as their basic views differed. The attack on the clergy also included a questioning of the right of the ecclesiastical courts to rule on matters of morality. The second movement was directed against the teaching of the church. As the Bible became better known, both through more biblical teaching and the availability of Wycliffe's translation, the teaching of the church was challenged by the teaching of the Bible.

Both movements were driven underground in the fourteenth century, coerced into silence by the power of church and state.

The medieval church

The clergy were divided into two parts – regular and secular. The secular clergy, who were under the jurisdiction of the bishop, included priests and prelates with cure of souls and a vast army of clerks engaged in all manner of occupations. The regular clergy were those living under some kind of rule – canons regular, monks and friars. The friars were entirely exempt from any kind of authority except the pope's; many of the monks were free from any kind of supervision by the bishops, and they all had their own organisations and officers independent of the rest of the church. Monks and friars looked for support to the pope, who made good use of them, while restricting more immediate local control. The bishops were supposedly appointed by election, but in fact by a connivance of king and pope. The law of England forbade the interference of the pope in these elections, but his permission had always to be sought. As the king usually wanted the bishops for councillors in affairs of state, he selected suitable men and the pope approved on condition that his men were appointed to other offices in the church. Both Edward III and Richard II found that the easiest way to secure the high places in the church for their friends was to act in alliance with Rome.

William of Wykeham, although superior to most of his fellow-bishops, is a good example of how these appointments were made. He rose in the favour of the court because of his abilities and his public services. As his usefulness to the King increased he was appointed to one benefice after another. His work was not concerned with spiritual things, but with building the castle at Windsor and keeping the palace accounts. He became Chancellor of England and Bishop of Winchester in the course of one month. Out of twentyfive bishops in England between 1376 and 1386, as many as thirteen held high secular office under the crown, and several others played an important part in politics. Sometimes they were sent abroad as ambassadors to foreign powers. The Bishop of Bath and Wells had been private chaplain to the Black Prince and had served him well as Chancellor of Gascony; the Bishop of Salisbury was similarly attached to John of Gaunt and served him as Chancellor of Lancaster. All these and others had risen to the bench by nomination of the king and the consent of the pope.

The close connection between the bench of bishops and the king was not a new departure in the church. William the Conqueror and Henry I, II and III trained and organised an effective bureaucracy in this way.

Seen from the point of view of the state, this may not have been too bad a system, but it had terrible effects upon the church. It meant that there was little or no spiritual supervision, and this was apparent in the church courts, where laymen suffered most.

But it is well to remember that the abuses noted by Chaucer and Langland were condemned strongly in a papal letter of the time, and some bishops were not too busy with their secular affairs to plead for reform — as did the Bishop of Durham in 1340 and the Archbishop of Canterbury in 1378.

The church was democratic in that it was the only institution by which a poor man's son could rise to eminence. Many bishops and even some archbishops came from the homes of the poor. Sometimes a promising serf was given his freedom to train for high office in the church and, subsequently, in the state. It is ironic that Langland criticises the church for this; he believed in gentle birth and did not approve of the church's carelessness about the birth or even the legitimacy of its clergy. Chaucer, however, thinks nothing of the fact that his Parson, the gentlest, sweetest saint in all his writings is brother to a ploughman:

'There was a plowman with him there, his brother.
Many a load of dung one time or other
He must have carted through the morning dew.'

The church opened up a career to all ranks and classes of people.

In yet another matter, the church demanded respect. It was the only educator of the poor, being responsible for founding places of education to which poor scholars were admitted.

The medieval church then, for all its mistakes, corruption and internal quarrels, its unpatriotic struggles and its lust for power, was still in theory and to a large extent also in practice, the poor man's church. It provided the background to everything that happened in the fourteenth century.

The need for reform

Enough has been said to show how much reform in church and state was needed. The Black Death of 1349, by emptying the land of labour, was the cause of the infamous Statute of Labourers, which for forty years tried to regulate and keep down the wages of the free-contracting labourer. The cost of the fruitless French wars rendered the country poorer with every dismal campaign. The death of the Black Prince in 1376 removed the last survivor of the age of chivalry. Had he lived, his sympathy for the poor might have relieved the worst effects of the Statute. The intolerable state of the nation without hope of improvement led inevitably to the rising of the Peasants Revolt in 1381, which, by its failure put back the cause of reform.

It was to such a land that Wycliffe spoke, and his words found echo in the hearts of his hearers. He began with the church.

2. Wycliffe, the Reformer

There is a picture in a psalter published in Bohemia in 1572 which gives a symbolic representation of Wycliffe among the Reformers. It shows Wycliffe striking the spark, John Huss (his Bohemian disciple) kindling the coal, and Luther brandishing the lighted torch. This is an accurate representation, for Huss was a faithful disciple of Wycliffe and did for his native Bohemia what Wycliffe had done for England even preserving the writings of his mentor when they were destoyed in England. It is also beyond dispute that the Hussites played an important part in hastening and influencing the German Reformation.

Oxford

Nothing is known of Wycliffe until he went to Oxford. Even his date of birth is uncertain — it was certainly before 1328! He entered Balliol College and embarked on a career destining him for office in church and state. Little is known of his student years, except that he took his master's degree in 1358. He was not a rich man and had therefore to use the means of the day to procure a living and to continue his studies. He was granted two benefices but was non-resident in both. Not a very propitious start for a Reformer! He was awarded his doctorate in 1372. It has been said that he was promised a lucrative post by Pope Gregory XI, but popes were notoriously bad at keeping their promises! He therefore did what any young clergyman would do at the time — he entered the service of the crown, and Edward III gave him the living of Lutterworth in Leicestershire which he held until his death.

His first public duty seems to have been in 1374 when he was appointed a member of a commission sent to Bruges to meet the papal representatives and lodge a complaint against the *curia* (or papal court) who claimed tribute as a feudal right, since King John had become a papal vassal. There was also another dispute involved. In writings produced that year Wycliffe argued that under certain conditions ecclesiastical property could be seized by the state. He based this upon his theories of 'lordship'. His first writing on the matter seems to be his *Determinatio* of 1374, but he developed his theses much more fully in the next two years in *De Dominio Divine* (On Divine Lordship, 1375) and *De Civili Dominio* (On Civil Lordship, 1376). These two books are based on lectures that he gave in Oxford after his return from Bruges.

Wycliffe had now established himself as a major thinker and he was at the centre of learning at Oxford.

On Divine Lordship

Wycliffe's orthodoxy was impeccable when he taught that God is the supreme Lord of all and all lordship is derived from him. Nor is this primacy of divine lordship abrogated, diminished, or nullified when God bestows an infinitesimal portion of it upon one of his human creatures. Such temporary loan of lordship is neither permanent nor unlimited, and is suited to the condition of the recipient.

> 'Hence, such a person is improperly called a
> lord, but is rather a steward of the supreme
> Lord. It is clear from this that every creature is
> a servant of the Lord,-possessing whatsoever
> he has of pure grace that he may husband it!'

On Civil Lordship

Wycliffe pressed on from this impeccable stance to argue that all power, civil and ecclesiastical, is held 'righteously' so long as the possessor remains in grace. Of course, powers are held 'naturally', but only the righteous hold them rightfully, or as Wycliffe puts it, 'from dignity and merit'. When applied to civil powers this was very acceptable to the church. It gave the priest power over the 'lords' and the pope very considerable secular power. But Wycliffe applied it also to the church, to the lords ecclesiastical.

In the last section of *On Civil Lordship,* Wycliffe turns to the relation of church and state, and denies the lawfulness of grants made to the church 'in perpetuity'. The ecclesiastical lords can only declare what God has done, but have no right themselves to make or receive a valid and perpetual grant. They are stewards, not masters.

Consequences were horrific. If these criteria were applied to the possessions of civil lords, the result would be an appalling and unquestioned power in the hands of the church. A rich lord could be declared not in grace and his property seized. Who could tell the state of a man's heart? Only the church could do that. But Wycliffe did not press the logic. He applied his criteria only to the church. There, if an ecclesiastical lord was not in grace, he was not the righteous possessor of property and should be deprived of it by the secular power. Vast sums of money or land had been left to the church for Masses for the souls of dead lords, and it was this wealth that was threatened by Wycliffe's proposals.

Wycliffe had long held the doctrine that Christ gave the church authority only over the spiritual, not the temporal, realm. He could quote a long list of highly respected church fathers to substantiate this. Moreover, he recalled Saint Francis with his insistence upon apostolic poverty as obligatory upon all priests. The chief cause of the church's ills, he maintained, lay in the great wealth of prelates, monks and priests. He traced the corruption of the church to the time of Constantine, when that emperor had allegedly endowed the papacy with temporal possessions and thus had 'poured poison into the church'.

The unworthy priest or prelate then, who manifests in his life lack of grace, should be deprived of his benefice. The church should do this, but because of the notorious corruption of the papacy located at that time in Avignon, and the scandalous Great Schism, in which there were two rival contenders for the papal throne, the state must undertake the role proper to a reformed church. Such teaching suited the civil lords, so long as it was not applied to them. John of Gaunt saw in it a way to add to his wealth and power. Together with the powerful Lord Percy he supported Wycliffe.

The riot in St Paul's

By 1377, John Wycliffe was known as one of the greatest scholars in the land, and his arguments for the disendowment of the church appealed both to greedy dukes and over-burdened taxpayers, to John of Gaunt and the citizens of London. His opinions spread over the country and with the connivance of John of Gaunt, he was invited to London to preach disendowment in the churches of the City. Wycliffe made the most of his opportunity. He found supporters among the citizens of London and a ready ear at court. He moved from church to church, preaching everywhere what laymen had long been thinking, but had never heard proclaimed with such boldness, nor defended with such learning. Meanwhile, the bishops and clergy of all England assembled in convocation were troubled at this contempt for their authority. Bishop Courtenay of London was particularly offended to have this priest from Oxford preaching so subversively in his diocese without authorisation. Archbishop Sudbury was reluctantly persuaded to summon Wycliffe before him at St Paul's.

On 19 February 1377, the bishops waited for the accused to arrive, seated in the Lady Chapel behind the altar. The London mob crowded the whole length of the aisle. At this moment they were not thinking of Wycliffe, although they held him in high regard. They were concerned about the political survival of their own great city, which was in danger. The ministers had that very week introduced a bill into Parliament which had the intention of taking the government of London out of the hands of the mayor and putting it into the hands of the King's Marshal, who was none other than Lord Percy. The citizens of London knew that by that bill their lives and liberties were at stake. They were after the blood of John and Gaunt and Lord Percy. The merits of the prisoner and his judges were not uppermost in their minds despite their moral support for Wycliffe.

Wycliffe arrived at the door of the great cathedral and moved slowly up the crowded aisle which was claimed to be the longest in Christendom. Four friars from Oxford, each representing one of their four orders, came with him to defend his doctrines. But the prisoner was not supported by logic and learning alone. By his side walked the great Duke of Lancaster, John of Gaunt; in front strode the King's Marshal, the northern lord who proposed to administer border law in the streets of London. With all the arrogance of a Percy he pushed the citizens of London out of the way to allow his patron and friend to pass unhindered. The arrogance continued as they moved to the Lady Chapel. Few have described this scene more vividly than GW Trevelyan:

> 'They had now reached the Lady Chapel where the conclave was sitting. The Duke and Lord took chairs for themselves and Percy bade Wycliffe be seated: "Since you have much to reply, you will need all the softer seat". Courtenay whose hot blood had been already stirred by the insolence the men had shown at their entry, cried out that the suggestion was impertinent, and that the accused should stand to give his answers. The two nobles swore that he should sit; Courtenay taking the proceedings

out of the hands of Archbishop Sudbury, who was glad enough to sit quiet, insisted that the prisoner should stand. The Duke, finding that he could not carry the point, broke out into abuse and threats. He would bring down the pride of all the Bishops of England; Courtenay need not put his trust in his parents the Earl and Countess of Devon, for they would have enough to do to take care of themselves. The Bishop made the obvious answer that he trusted in God and not in his high connections. The next moment the Londoners had broken in on the proceedings with wild cries of vengence, and a general melée ensued between the citizens and the Duke's guard. The assembly broke up in confusion, and the prisoner was carried off by his supporters, whether in triumph or in retreat it was hard to tell. Of Wycliffe's share in the proceedings it can only be asserted that he made no noticeable interference, and that he lost no popularity in London on account of the events of that day. What he thought of it all we can never even guess. Whether he had wished the Duke to accompany him must remain a mystery. He does not mention the scene in any of his works, though he speaks much of his later persecutions. In the roaring crowd of infuriated lords, bishops and citizens, he stood silent and stands silent still'

What followed was a riot in the cathedral, with a hunt for Duke and Lord, as chaos broke out in London. The rioting had nothing to do with Wycliffe. The citizens were not defending or attacking his reforms of the church; they were defending their threatened liberties. Both the Duke of Lancaster and Lord Percy narrowly escaped with their lives. John Wycliffe was never really in danger.

The papal bull

The summoning of Wycliffe to appear before the English Bishops in St Paul's, which ended in such a fiasco, was at the instigation of Bishop Courtenay without any reference to the Pope. Pope Gregory was busy returning from Avignon to Rome, where he found the Lateran Palace in ruins and unsafe. He established the papacy where the Vatican now stands and near enough to the Castle of St Angelo to escape there in times of danger. There he heard news of Bishop Courtenay's failure and of Wycliffe's doctrine.

In the latter part of May, he issued a series of bulls (papal edicts) to various authorities in England, ordering the arrest of Wycliffe. The nineteen heresies he imputed to him were mostly political. There were some obscure points of doctrine which a man like Wycliffe could easily have answered. But what really worried Pope Gregory was the political implications of what Wycliffe was proclaiming so clearly. He was declared a heretic because he was standing for England against Rome, for the state against the church. The bull asserted that he had declared against the power of the pope to loose and to bind and had said that excommunication, when it was unjust, had no value and no effect. Wycliffe, he said, had pronounced it the duty of the state to secularise the property of the church when it became too rich, in order to purify her. There were many other points, such as that any priest could administer sacraments reserved for bishops alone, and that the saints were in possession of all things.

Reading through the accusations it does sound as though Wycliffe was teaching both a form of Presbyterianism and also, in political matters, a primitive form of Communism. It also looked as though he were anticipating Henry VIII in his advocacy of a national church. Almost all the points of which he was accused could be found in one form or another in his writings, but they constituted a plea for reform rather than heresy.

Wycliffe had the people and the government on his side. The people saw him as a national champion against the papacy, and the government which met in October 1377 was violently antipapal. He also articulated the national feeling against the abuses of the church. Few saw how far he was leading them, but the majority were happy with the general direction of his proposed reforms. When the Houses of Parliament had brought back the policy of the reforming Good Parliament which the king, influenced by John of Gaunt, had so shamefully ignored, Wycliffe appeared in person and had a rousing, one must say, anti-papal reception. He presented to the members a defence of his 'heresies' and was listened to with respect. His defence, however, was so technical that any honest knight of the shire who had tried to understand him would have been mightily puzzled! But he was their champion that day.

The bishops did nothing. They would have been foolish to obey the Pope and bring an accusation against the favourite of the governors of the kingdom. The disasters of that year, 1377, had brought home to all the evils of papal taxation. The Rolls of Parliament record the complaint that 'the French ecclesiastics holding benefices in England use their endowments against the English arms in France'. Even more extensive was the export of money by means of the Pope's direct taxation. The young King Richard on the advice of his Council sought means to prevent the export of money to pay for the Pope's wars in Italy. Wycliffe, although under the ban of the Pope's bulls, was asked by the King to draw up an answer to the question, 'Whether the Realm of England can legitimately, when the necessity of repelling invasion is imminent, withhold the treasure of the Realm that it be not sent to foreign parts, although the Pope demand it under pain of censure and in virtue of obedience due to him'.

Of course, Wycliffe took the opportunity to deal with other questions while he was about it and was duly silenced for going too far. But the fact that he could be asked such a thing at all while still under the ban of the papal bulls shows how popular were his doctrines. So far as the question was concerned, he firmly asserted the limited authority of the pope to collect only charity. He also made his proposals for a national church independent of Rome. While the Bishops did nothing, Wycliffe issued his answer to the nineteen charges of heresy. He did not entirely repudiate the power of the pope, but he did reject the power of a bad pope, such as he believed Gregory to be.

It was not until 18 December that the bishops acted upon the Pope's orders by demanding that the Oxford authorities arrest John Wycliffe. The bull that Oxford had received from the Vatican had put them into some difficulty. Not only was there a strong party in favour of Wycliffe and his views, but it was against the common law of England to arrest a king's subject in obedience to a papal bull. But the Pope had ordered this arrest on pain of the university losing all its privileges. So they took counsel and solved the matter by ordering John Wycliffe to stay in his lodgings in Black Hall and not go out because, as the Vice-Chancellor said, 'he wished no one else to arrest him'. Meanwhile, the Chancellor took the advice of all the masters of theology and declared publicly that Wycliffe's propositions which had been condemned, 'were true, though they sounded badly to the ear'.

Wycliffe's second trial

Encouraged by the courteous and supportive behaviour of the university, Wycliffe agreed to appear before the Papal Commissioners (Bishop Courtenay and Archbishop Sudbury) at Lambeth early in 1378. This time there was no powerful John of Gaunt by his side, but he was in a much stronger position without him. The issue at stake, however, was not really whether Wycliffe was a heretic or not, but whether the Pope had jurisdiction over the laws of England. The King's councillors had sought his advice and constituted him their champion against the pope.

Just before the trial began, Sir Lewis Clifford arrived with a message from the widow of the Black Prince, now the Queen-mother, forbidding the bishops to take any 'decided action against the prisoner'. At an early stage of the trial a London mob broke up the proceedings by entering the chapel at Lambeth and exhibiting violent support for their champion. Thomas Walsingham, the monkish chronicler, was outraged: 'In this way that slippery John Wycliffe deluded his inquisitors, mocked the bishops, and escaped them by the favour and care of the Londoners, although all his propositions are clearly heretical and depraved.'

This trial at Lambeth had once and for all (except briefly under Mary's reign) settled the question of papal authority in the realm of England and kept out the Inquisition which so scarred Spain and Italy. Although tax collectors and pardon mongers continued, the horrors of the Inquisition were kept from England.

The right of sanctuary

Later in the same year, 1378, Wycliffe was involved in the dispute over the right of sanctuary in churches for wilful criminals. Two knights — Shakell and Haule — had received sanctuary in Westminster Abbey. On 11 August, the governor of the Tower of London, from which they had escaped, came to recover his prisoners in the teeth of church privileges. The party that went to recover them included officials from the Tower in performance of their duty, and private persons from the court, acting in connivance with John of Gaunt. They succeeded in arresting Shakell without much scandal, after some arguments. Haule was in the Abbey Church itself, attending Mass. The soldiers entered the church and laid hands on him. He drew his sword and beat them off, but in the chase that followed he was killed in the church and his body dragged down the steps and thrown outside.

Archbishop Sudbury, usually quite timid, was roused to action. He excommunicated the governor of the Tower and all who had aided and abetted him, specifically excluding the King, his mother and the Duke of Lancaster. The government defended the right of its officers to execute their duty. The King ordered the reading of the excommunication to be stopped; the Abbot forbade the reconsecration of the Abbey Church and forbade the monks to continue their worship there. The Abbot was summoned before the King and Bishop Courtenay read the excommunication at St Paul's Cross. The affair had thus given rise to a serious and open quarrel between church and state.

In October, Parliament assembled, not in Westminster, but at Gloucester, and debated the matter of Sanctuary. While repudiating the killing of a knight in the church, and incidentally also an officer of the church, the government maintained the right of the King's officers to make the arrest in church. The right of sanctuary had become a public nuisance. Any criminal escaping from justice for felony or even murder had only to reach the nearest church and he was perfectly safe. The Parliament at Gloucester called in certain doctors of theology and civil law to assist in this debate. One of those brought in was John Wycliffe. Fortunately the paper he read has been preserved.

Wycliffe's attitude to sanctuary

Wycliffe declared that he would not defend the abominable slaughter of Haule, although he pointed out that the knight himself had been the first to draw sword in the church. What he undertook to defend was the action of the officers in entering the church to make the arrest. He tried to show that the privilege of sanctuary, although hallowed by long custom, was illegal.

As usual, he started with the Bible. God established cities of refuge for accidental homicide (Exodus 21: 12-14), not for wilful crime. The right of sanctuary was a flagrant defiance of justice; without justice the state could not stand. The argument of 'mercy' was hypocritical. It was not mercy to rob a creditor of his due. The clergy did not forgive men debts due to them. False piety and unjust pity are to be condemned.

Wycliffe devotes much of his paper to a consideration of the privilege of sanctuary from the point of view of the church itself. Such privileges as these only make the clergy forgetful of the true service of God. He had already maintained earlier that the clergy would be improved and spiritualised by their loss of worldly goods. Now he maintained that the loss of worldly privileges would be no less beneficial!

The result of all this argument was not very impressive. It led to one mild statute, passed eventually at Westminster in 1379, whereby the fraudulent debtor taking sanctuary was to be summoned to the door of the church. This was to be done once a week until thirty-one days had passed. If at the end, he did not appear, judgement was to go against him and his goods were to be seized. This mild measure was scarcely an interference with the right of sanctuary.

The lordship of the king

This miserably inadequate statute could hardly be expected to satisfy Wycliffe who felt it to be a poor basis for reconciliation between church and state, as well as an avoidance of reform. His hope now turned to the king. His pamphlet, *De Officio Regis,* brought out in the same year as the statute, 1379, called upon the king to exercise his proper powers to reform the church. He maintained that the church should be under the supervision of secular powers for its own good. It could not reform itself and bishops, cardinals and popes had all failed to amend conspicuous evils. It was the proper office of the king to compel the bishops to look to the state of the clergy in their dioceses and remove notoriously immoral and inefficient pastors. The king, again through the bishops, should force incumbents to live in their parishes; he should prevent the appointment of ignorant priests and compel all clerks to study.

The extraordinary thing about this pamphlet is that it foreshadowed the peculiarity of the English Reformation under Tudors and Stuarts. The revolutionary character of the pamphlet made it ineffective in its day. The medieval view of church and state was one of separation: one did not interfere with the other. When this was breached, it was always the church that interfered with the state. Wycliffe was proposing in this pamphlet an English church governed by the king and coextensive with the state.

Transubstantiation

The critical moment passed and Wycliffe was quiet for two years. During 1379 and 1380, he formulated the theory, and taught in his lecture room at Oxford, that the doctrine of transubstantiation was contrary to the teaching of the New Testament. In this he was attacking the central doctrine of the Catholic Church in his day. The church had not always taught this miracle of the changing of the bread and wine on the altar into the body and blood of Christ, a supernatural power given to priests alone. Wycliffe found that it was not believed by the early fathers of the church and that it ran counter to the teaching of the New Testament.

He saw the value of the doctrine for the church, who could dominate the laity by withholding the body and blood of Christ: they held in supreme sanction in an age of faith. He argued that the 'orthodox' view of the Eucharist was the cause of idolatry; the people made the host their God. He further declared that nothing was more horrible to him than the idea that every celebrating priest created the body of Christ. The Mass was, in his view, a false miracle invented for worldly purposes to give the church power over the people.

The storm arose at once and Wycliffe never for an instant shrank from its fury. John of Gaunt hurried to Oxford in person and ordered him to be silent. He refused, and so sacrificed the support of the most powerful man in the kingdom. He did not go further than to condemn the doctrine of transubstantiation. The Eucharist was for him a mystery; he thought that the body of Christ was in some manner there, but the bread was present also. He did not proceed to attack the other sacraments of the church, although his followers did. He was lukewarm about the saving qualities of ceremonies, prayers and pardons and pointed out that there was an alternative road to salvation − a godly life. He thought the religious world had been led astray by formulas and had forgotten the essence of Christianity. The direct relation of an individual to God, without these interventions, was at the heart of the teaching. The new covenant in Jeremiah 31 was nearer to the truth of Christianity than was the magic of the Mass.

Christian worship

In his controversial essay *On the Eucharist* in which he had denied the doctrine of transubstantiation, Wycliffe applies a biblical study of the Eucharist to the general worship of the people:

> 'Just as when the cup is seen we break forth
> into profound worship, so also when the
> consecrated host is seen we do the same, not
> on account of the fact that that very cup has
> been consecrated by the priest, but because of
> the excellent sacrament hidden in the vessel.
> Thus when we see the host we ought to believe,

not that it is itself the body of Christ, but that the body of Christ is sacramentally concealed in it. And this is the meaning of the Church when it sings:

> *Beneath these many forms we see*
> *Signs only, not reality;*
> *The wonder lies concealed'.*

In another pamphlet, *De Ecclesia* (On the church) he maintained that the test of a ritual's value was the degree to which it increased the devotion of the people. Thus he found that intoning and elaborate singing took the mind off the meaning of the prayer. He quoted from Saint Augustine — a quote which later became very popular with his followers — the dictum 'as oft as the song delighteth me more than what is sung, so oft I acknowledge that I trespass grievously'.

By the same standards, he judged that the splendid buildings and gaudy decoration of churches distracted the minds of the worshippers. At a time when Gothic architecture was becoming increasingly elaborate, and the singing far removed from the simple beauty of the Gregorian chant, there were many who sought simplicity in worship. Wycliffe gave voice to this need and his followers put it into practice, preferring 'caves and woods' to the spendour of the Decorated style or elaborate music. They sought to worship God, not to attend a performance by the priest. These new 'English heretics', inspired by Wycliffe, gave a distinctively 'Protestant' character to their worship. They insisted upon the greater importance of preaching over ceremonies. Preaching, they maintained, was of more benefit to the laity than any sacrament. The sermon was the special weapon of these early reformers. Much of Wycliffe's English writing reads like sermons, and these weapons distinguished his 'poor priests'.

Their rivals were the friars, who could never be accused

of sloth. The parish priest may be idle, the monk may be out of touch with the world, the bishops may be secularised, but the friars were actively engaged in preaching throughout the country. They emptied the churches of their congregations and were particularly influential with the women. Wycliffe accused the friars of preaching to amuse people and to win their money, making up for real earnestness by telling stories which were more popular than edifying. He wanted an entirely different class of preacher, one who would call people to repentance, and make the sermon the great instrument for reformation of life and manners. To Wycliffe, preaching seemed the most effectual means to rouse people to a sense of their personal relation with God, and of the conseqent importance of their every action. Absolution, masses, pardons and penance commuted for money were so many ways of avoiding any real feeling of responsibility.

Worship of images and prayers to the saints

Wycliffe never anticipated the iconoclasm to which his views ultimately led in the sixteenth century. He respected the images in the churches and thought they could be aids to devotion. He attacked only the misuse of images. His test was always what led to truer devotion.

In the same way he did not attack prayers to the saints, although he preferred a general respect for saintliness to attachment to individual saints. If prayer to a saint helped the worship of Christ and led to better living, then Wycliffe had nothing against it. But the misuses to which saint worship and relics were put filled him with anger. He certainly put little store on whether Rome canonised a saint or not. 'The example of our great predecessors can be honoured without an edict from Rome'.

His treatment of the Virgin Mary was sensitive and devout. He held her up as an example to be followed, especially by women. He has an interesting treatise called *Ave Maria,* in which he describes her exemplary life in language full of sympathy and beauty. But he does not advise people to pray to her. He does not speak either in praise or in condemnation of the image of the Virgin, which then looked down from every church in the land.

Wycliffe was a man of his time and had spent much of his life in the piety of his age. It would have been insensitive of him to engage in a tirade against idolatry, but he mentions the mistaken use of images as part of other superstitious practices attached to the popular cult of saints. He put this on the same level as the foolish adoration of relics, the costly decoration of shrines, and other ways in which pilgrims wasted their time and money. Against those who lived by encouraging such superstitions, Wycliffe waged implacable war. The monks and friars attracted his violent condemnation. He believed that all should belong to the sect of Christ and that there was no warrant in Scripture for people binding themselves to any other rule than that of the gospel which bound all Christ's people. The monks and friars offended in this matter. They claimed to be 'the religious', more dear to God than other people. But their rule was of earthly making.

The reform of church government

Wycliffe saw that the only hope for the church was to reform its structures, although he had no alternative church order to suggest. He cared little for ordination or apostolic succession. He taught people to look for the real worth of a man, irrespective of his position in the church. 'For crown and cloth make no priest', he wrote, 'nor the emperor's bishop with his words, but power that Christ giveth, and thus by life are priests known.' His language was often violent, but he was taking on the whole medieval church, which did not hesitate to use violence in word and deed against him and his followers. He wanted a church free from all these pious hypocrites who lived off the poor and kept them in the bondage of superstition. Wycliffe knew what he was doing and did it as a duty, not as an intellectual pastime. He was not a man for compromise or soft words that conceal the truth. He wanted peace, but not false peace: 'There is very peace and false peace, and they be full diverse. Very peace is grounded in God . . . false peace is grounded on rest with our enemies, when we assent to them without again-standing'.

The pope had no place in Wycliffe's free church of all Christians. His argument was plain: 'If thou say that Christ's Church must have a head here in the earth, sooth it is, for Christ is head, that must be here with his Church unto the day of doom'. But this complete repudiation of papal authority was the last step in a long process. Until the time of the Great Schism he did no more than insist upon the fallibility of the pope and attack any deviation from the divine law. He thought Gregory a bad pope, but he welcomed the accession of Urban VI as a reforming pope. Then from Avignon came a rival, Pope Clement, and he and Urban issued excommunications at one another. Only then did Wycliffe deny all papal authority over the church.

In place of the absolute authority of a human and fallible pope he set up the authority of the Bible. This doctrine was most carefully worked out in a treatise which he wrote in the year of the Great Schism, 1378. *'On the Truth of the Holy Scripture'* asserts and defends the absolute superiority of the scriptural doctrine over scholastic theology or papal supremacy. The Bible alone is the supreme organ of divine revelation; the church's tradition, pronouncements of the councils, papal decrees, and all other expositions of Christian doctrine must be tested on the scriptural touchstone. All truth is contained in the Scriptures. They are divinely inspired in all their parts, and they alone are a sufficient guide in all matters, religious and secular. All Christians must know them and read them in their own language. 'May God move lords and bishops to stand up for the knowing of His law'.

3. The Peasants Revolt of 1381

Although John Wycliffe directed his attention primarily to the reform of the church, there was no mistaking the consequences of what he taught for the reform of society. As we have seen in our own day in Latin America, there comes a time when theoretical ideas are matched by a glimpse of the possibility of actual change, and then a spark is set off. The communists have called this situation 'conscientisation' and they have worked upon it to bring about revolution. When there is abject poverty, the people may be docile, until they become conscious that they are poor and need not be. In Wycliffe's day, the church had condemned outright slavery, but the situation of the villein within the manorial system was accepted. As this system changed, and hired labour took the place of labour due in exchange for land, the idea of personal freedom was brought forcibly before the peasants. At the same time, the common origin of mankind in Adam and Eve, which was not seen mythologically, but historically, gave rise to the famous catchword:

When Adam delved and Eve span,
Who was then the gentleman?

Again, as in Latin America today, those who stirred up these aspirations towards equality and freedom were the local priests who were most in touch with the people. In many cases they shared their poverty. If in addition they were affected by Wycliffe's teaching of the 'rightful' holding of property only by those who were 'in grace', they were the more stimulated to reform both church and society.

John Ball

The principal agitator in the peasant rising of 1381 was a chaplain and religious zealot called John Ball. For twenty years he had been going round the country like John the Baptist, attacking church and state alike. His principal target was the serfdom of the villein. He did not get his ideas from Wycliffe. In fact he had been following his radical role long before John Wycliffe was of any importance in church or politics. Neither did Wycliffe learn from him, because he reached his conclusions from quite different sources. Wycliffe's thinking was essentially biblical and he found all his sources in the Old Testament prophets and the gospels. John Ball, however, prepared the way for the widespread influence of Wycliffe's teaching.

John Ball had once been a priest in the north of England, but finally became an agitator in London. It is said that in later years he adopted Wycliffe's views on the Eucharist and there are many other points in which the two held views in common. One thing that distinguished them was Wycliffe's distaste for violence. As in the disputes over the right of sanctuary he had accepted the right of the officers to enter the church but condemned the violence used, he now accepted the rights of peasants to freedom and justice, but deplored the use of violence. John Ball, however, was prepared to believe that the peasants would never get their rights except by force. Froissart, in his *Chronicles,* describes John Ball as an agitator for a kind of communism:

> 'He (John Ball) was accustomed every Sunday,
> as the people were coming out of the church,
> to preach to them in the market-place and
> assemble a crowd around him, to whom he
> would say, "My good friends, things cannot
> go well in England, nor ever will until
> everything shall be in common; when there

shall be neither vassal nor lord and all distinctions levelled, when the lords shall be no more masters than ourselves. How ill have they used us? And for what reason do they thus hold us in bondage? Are we not all descended from the same parents, Adam and Eve? And what can they show or what reasons give, why they should be more masters than ourselves except perhaps in making us labour and work for them to spend? They are clothed in velvets and rich stuffs, ornamented with ermine and other furs, while we are forced to wear poor clothes. They have handsome seats and manors, when we must brave the wind and rain in our labours in the field; but it is from our labour they have wherewith to support their pomp. We are called slaves, and if we do not perform our services we are beaten.'''

Froissart writes as one with little sympathy for the rising, and perhaps exaggerates John Ball's inflammatory style of oratory. Certainly there was little demand, when it came to the point, for 'all things in common'. The peasants were not seeking to establish a communist form of government, but simply asking for fair treatment. Their demands were very modest indeed: personal freedom and the commutation of all forms of labour for a rent of four pence an acre. When this was granted, most of the peasants were prepared to go home. Even those who were not had no plans for communism. Their further claims were for the disendowment of the church, free use of forests, abolition of game laws and of outlawry.

Wycliffe's opposition to the friars

Although the preaching of 'all things in common' was not the message heard by most peasants, there seems little doubt that the itinerant friars put it about. Langland says of them,

They preach men of Plato and prove it by Seneca,
That all things under Heaven ought to be in common;
And yet he lieth, as I live, that to the unlearned
  so preacheth

There were others beside the friars who were itinerant preachers. Wycliffe had not yet organised his Poor Preachers to go forth and preach the true gospel, but men who drew some of their doctrine from him carried his early teaching far and wide. Wycliffe himself had lost all interest in the theory of the righteous holding all property in common and was more and more interested in church affairs.

However, he saw the danger of the friars, who preached such teaching not out of conviction but for gain. D'Aubigné in his *The Reformation in England* sees this opposition to the friars as one of the reasons why Wycliffe started his Poor Priests. He quotes Wycliffe as saying 'If begging friars stroll over the country, . . . we must do for God's glory what they do to fill their wallets, and form a vast itinerant organisation to convert souls to Jesus Christ'.

Friars and followers of Wycliffe had some points in common in their teaching, but their aims were different. Many of the friars courted popularity among the crowds, although of course many were sincerely concerned about the growing poverty and injustice in the land. The followers of Wycliffe cared deeply about the truth. They were concerned less to change society than to change people's hearts. They were not seeking the 'purification' of the Kingdom of England, but the advance of the Kingdom of Christ. Both were effective in giving new revolutionary fire — whether they intended it or not — to the dissatisfied peasants, and contributed in this way to the rising of 1381.

Chronicles of the rising

Various Chroniclers have provided very detailed accounts of what happened in the Peasants Revolt. They are not unbiassed and most were horrified by the sight of the power wielded by the peasants. All were in favour of law and order but, having said this, we must be grateful for such vivid reporting.

The rising spread throughout the country and at times seemed uncoordinated. There were named leaders, but no national organisation. The savage poll taxes, of which there were three enactments between 1377 and 1381, caused such hardship as to make a rising desperate. Isolated acts of resistance to the activities of the tax commissioners occurred in May 1381. The various Chroniclers are not always consistent but the general outline is clear. Open defiance of the tax commissioners apparently led to serious conflict first in three marshland villages near Brentwood and later spread to other parts of Essex. The peasants of Essex showed considerable cohesion and soon developed a sense of purpose. But the Chroniclers seem most alarmed when the revolt spread to Kent. The decision to march on London was crucial, and threw the parliament which had enacted the poll tax laws into near panic. Under the guidance of Wat Tyler, John Ball and other leaders, the peasants of Kent were united − as they would never be again − and were assured of success as they made their way from Canterbury to London, on 11 and 12 June 1381.

Assessment of the rising

As the rising swept the country, many who had approved of the demands to abolish the poll taxes were dubious of the methods used. It may be assumed that Wycliffe disapproved of the violence. It was always his way to prefer words to weapons, and persuasion to coercion. But little remains of his comments upon the Peasants'

Revolt, although his Lollards were much involved. However, Wycliffe's clear statements about private judgement with regard to the church: 'we claim to be exempt from this authority in this respect, and to be left to the guidance of reason and Scripture', was bound to have its effect. GM Trevelyan, in his earliest book, assesses the Revolt in more kindly terms than the hostile Chroniclers and implicates Wycliffe.

'The general tone of the Rising was that of
Christian Democracy. The chief agitator
(John Ball) who had spread discontent and
formulated the theories of rebellion was a
priest, and friars and Lollards alike were
accused with more or less truth, of carrying on
Ball's work. In the Rising itself, several
parsons of poor parishes put themselves at the
head of their congregations and revenged on
society the wrongs that they had endured. But
the vast majority of the actual leaders were not
men of the Church. Those who called out their
neighbours in the towns and villages of
England, when the Rising was well on foot,
were generally laymen.'

But the implication is only directed at the logic of Wycliffe's teaching. He showed no sympathy to the levellers.

Wycliffe left no doubt as to his views about the proper relations between master and servant. Both had obligations to each other. He continually emphasised the rights of property and the duty of performing services even to sinful lords. Christians must render legal dues without question of their equity. His own theory of 'lordship', so dangerous to the proprietary rights of the wicked, remained still-born in the *De Dominio Civili* and did not reappear in any of his later Latin writings, nor any of his English tracts. Popular preachers were calling upon villeins to withdraw their services because of the wickedness of their masters. This was surely in keeping with Wycliffe's earlier theory. But now that it had become a practical question and the issues of law and order were at stake, he saw the dangers to society and denounced in practice what he had declared in theory. Or rather, he denounced the most crude and levelling influences. FD Matthew, in his valuable collection of Wycliffe's English works (1880), uncovers the clearest statement of the Reformer's assessment: 'The fiend moveth some men to say that Christian men should not be servants or thralls to heathen lords, sith they ben false to God and less worthy than Christian men; neither to Christian lords, for they ben brethren in kind, and Jesus Christ bought men on the Cross and made them free. But against this heresy Paul writeth in God's law'.

Wycliffe is clearly uncomfortable because the leveller's argument is logical and his only authority is the references in Paul's letters about slaves being obedient to their masters. But he is really defending his 'Poor Priests' who were being accused of encouraging violence and lawlessness. He continues, 'But yet, some men that ben out of charity, slander Poor Priests with this error, that servants or tenants may lawfully withhold rents or services from their lords, when lords ben openly wicked in their living'. But if Wycliffe could defend the rights of the lords, he was not slow in denouncing the wrongs done to the peasants.

> Strifes, contests and debates ben used in our land, for lords striven with their tenants to bring them in thraldom more than they shoulden by reason and charity. Also lords many times do wrongs to poor men by extortions and unreasonable amercements and unreasonable taxes, and take poor men's goods and payen (money) not therefore but with tallies (sticks), and despisen them and menace

and sometimes beat them when they ask their pay. And thus lords devour poor men's goods in gluttony and waste and pride, and they perish for mischief and hunger and thirst and cold, and their children also. And if their rent be not readily paid their beasts ber distressed, and they pursued without mercy, though they ben never so poor and needy. And so in a manner they eat and drink poor men's flesh and blood, and ben man-quellers, as God complaineth by his prophets'[2]

It was Wycliffe's large view of the social problems of his day which enabled him to speak with moderation of the rising when it was over.

The rebels in London

All the Chroniclers of the Peasants' Revolt agree that the climax of this astounding event was the three days in Corpus Christi Week, 13, 14, 15 June 1381 in London. Then, according to Froissart, apparently quoting the words of Richard II, 'the heritage and realm of England were near lost'. Looking back, the rising was doomed to failure. No band of medieval English rebels could retain their coherence for long. The events were vivid, dramatic and tragic and to this day many questions remain unanswered. That Thursday, Friday and Saturday in one week gave Londoners the most exciting and most disorderly time that the medieval city had ever seen. The full story has been told by many Chroniclers, not without some contradictions, and there are records of trials that can also yield some information. Eye-witnesses agree on certain striking events: the sack of the Savoy on Thursday afternoon, the Mile End conference and the execution of Archbishop Sudbury and others on the Friday, the young King's visit to Westminster Abbey on the Saturday morning, shortly before the famous confrontation of King and people at Smithfield.

An eye-witness account

The Anonimalle Chronicles edited by V.H. Galbraith (Manchester 1927) covers the period 1333-1381. The author appears to have been an eye-witness during many of the events of those three days. I have depended very much upon his account in telling the following story of the Revolt.

On Wednesday (12 June 1381), the peasants from Kent arrived in Southwark, the site of the Marshalsea. This was a debtor's prison notorious for the great numbers confined there in inhuman conditions. There were also some there accused of criminal offences. The attitude of the Kentish rebels to this prison was much the same as later the French revolutionaries would have to the Bastille. It was a symbol of power unjustly used against them. There were about 60,000 Kentish peasants and they made short work of the prison and its outlying buildings. They released the prisoners and destroyed the homes of the jurors and professional informers, as well as the mansion of the Marshal, John Imworth.

About the same time, the Essex peasants came to Lambeth and either they or their counterparts from Kent sacked the Archbishop's Palace there. Whoever it was they entered the building and destroyed property and the registers and chancery rolls.

Next day, the feast of Corpus Christi, the Essex rebels moved to Highbury. Either then or the next morning, they set fire to the house of the Master of the Hospital of St John.

Meanwhile the Kent contingent destroyed a brothel near London Bridge. The reason for the venom against the brothel seems to have been its connection with the mayor of London who had filled it with Flemish women to his profit. They attempted to cross the bridge into London, but the mayor obstructed their passage by putting a chain across the bridge. The people of Southwark joined the rebels and demanded, with threats, that the mayor allow them to enter. Whether from treachery or fear, the keepers let down the chains and the multitude flooded into London, while 'the religious as well as the parsons and vicars devoutly went into procession to pray to God for peace'. Meanwhile, undeterred, the crowd came to Fleet Street without doing much harm on the way. The citizens of London were also playing their part, setting fire to and destroying the Savoy. In Fleet Street, the rebels from Kent opened the doors of the Fleet prison and burnt some shops and houses. They went on to the Temple, destroying all they could and, in the Temple church, seized all the books, rolls and remembrances, carrying them out and burning them in the high road.

The crowd seemed by now to be set on attacking the church authorities, but on the whole they did not attack churches. The Savoy was sacked, as were all the houses that belonged to the Knights Templars of St John. There is a lively account of their attack on the palace of the Bishop of Chester, where they discovered his cellar and drank their full. It was therefore as a drunken mob that they went into the Savoy and set fire to all the cloths, coverlets and beds they could find. They burnt the hall with its chambers. Londoners remembered the explosions and fires in the palace of the Savoy for many years to come. The pattern continued into Westminster, with the crowd opening prisons and destroying wealthy houses, particularly those belonging to church dignitaries or the hated Duke of Lancaster. There were some cases of personal revenge, such as when Roger Legget was dragged from the alter of St Martin-le-Grand and beheaded in Cheap Street. But there were few executions on that day.

After an unsuccessful attempt to see the King at the Tower of London, the crowd rested. The young King had seen, from the turret of the great tower, the burning of the Savoy and the Hospital of Clerkenwell and several houses of famous subjects. He was troubled, but not afraid, this was really his chance to show courage and he did. He called the lords about him into the chamber and asked what he should do. They gave him no counsel, so he told them what he would do. He ordered the mayor of the city to command the sheriffs and aldermen to have it cried within their wards that everyone between fifteen and sixty should come to Mile End to meet their King. This meeting was to be on Friday. Meanwhile the King remained in the Tower. He attempted to contact some of the peasants who were staying nearby. He told them to go to their homes and he would pardon them all. With one voice they said that they would not go home until they had captured the traitors within the tower, and obtained charters to free them from all manner of serfdom. The King responded by drafting a royal bill:

> 'Richard, king of England and France, gives
> great thanks to his good commons, for that
> they have so great a desire to see and maintain
> their king; and he grants them pardon for all
> manner of trespasses and misprisions and
> felonies done up to this hour, and wills and
> commands that every one should now return to
> his own home: He wills and commands that
> everyone should put his grievances in writing,
> and have them sent to him; and he will provide
> with the aid of his loyal lords and his good
> council, such remedies as shall be profitable
> both to him and to them, and to the kingdom'.

He sealed this solemn statement and sent it to the rebels by the hand of two of his knights. Meanwhile he waited in the tower. The people heard the bill read and reacted by saying that it was nothing but a trifle and a mockery.

The encounters with the King

The King had proclaimed that he would meet the rebels at Mile End. By now their strength was about 100,000. Some remained watching the Tower, to ensure that traitors like the Archbishop of Canterbury should not escape the judgement they had in store for him. He did not escape. On the Friday, some went to Mile End. At 7a.m. the King arrived with his mother and several companions – earls, knights and the mayor of London. The people paid respect to the King with the words, 'Welcome our Lord King Richard, if it pleases you, and we will not have any other king but you'.

There is a difference of opinion about whether Wat Tyler was there. On other occasions he behaved so rudely towards the King that the leader at Mile End seems another person. But it was he who made the demands, now familiar, which illustrate the cause of the rising. First they wanted to seize all traitors and try them before beheading them. The King granted this, provided they would guarantee a proper legal trial. Then they asked that there should be no serfs, nor should anyone make homage or any type of service to a lord. Instead they should pay four pence per acre for their land. They asked that no person should serve another except by his own free will. The King agreed to all this and they made their way to the Tower to seize the traitors there. The main target was the Archbishop of Canterbury. It was a terrible Friday in London with 140 to 160 people beheaded. Foreigners of all kind were in danger and Flemings were given short shift. On the Saturday, they tried John Imworth, the marshall of Marshalsea. He was dragged, apparently in the presence of the King, from Westminster Hall to Cheap Street where he was beheaded.

The King arrived in Westminster Abbey about 3p.m. with 200 people accompanying him. After prayers and confession, he proclaimed that all should meet him at Smithfield, by St Bartholomew's Church.

This time Wat Tyler was certainly the leader, and he swaggered before the King. A valet shouted at him and in a scuffle with the mayor, William of Walworth, he was mortally wounded. When Tyler cried for vengeance, the rebels bent their bows. The King, with great courage, rode out towards them in open field and called upon them to meet him in the field of St John, Clerkenwell. Meanwhile the mayor assembled a large number of armed men. Thus, when the King reached the open field he was backed by a strong company for the first time. The mayor had the wounded Wat Tyler brought out to the middle of Smithfield and beheaded him. The rising collapsed. The rebels begged the King for mercy and he granted it. Some fled, others were escorted through London to avoid further damage, until they had passed over London Bridge. Troubles did not completely cease in other parts of the country. But the rebels now had their charter, of which John Wycliffe would approve, even though he disapproved of the way they got it.

The Royal Charter

The text of the charter, which one of the Chronicles quaintly describes as 'Royal Charter concerning the manumission of the rustics', is of great importance as defining the right to freedom of the people of England. It was not always kept to the letter, but it provided a basis for many in the years to come, as they sought to maintain the freedom of the English people.

> 'Richard, by the grace of God, king of
> England and France, the lord of Ireland, to all
> his bailiffs and faithful men to whom these
> present letters come, greetings. Know that by
> our special grace we have manumitted all our
> liegemen, subjects and others of the county of
> Hertfordshire; and we have freed and quitted
> each of them from bondage by the present
> letters. We also pardon our said liegemen and
> subjects for all felonies, acts of treason,
> transgressions and extortions performed by
> them or any one of them in whatsoever way.
> We also withdraw sentences of outlawry

declared against them or any of them because of these offences. And we hereby grant our complete peace to them and each of them. In testimony of which we order these letters of ours to be made patent. Witnessed by myself at London on 15 June in the fourth year of my reign'.

The reference to Hertfordshire is because this version comes from the Chronicle of Thomas Walsingham of St Albans. This very general amnesty did not prevent the people of St Albans rioting when they returned home.

Suppression

The killing of Wat Tyler and the subsequent execution of the most notorious rebel leaders (Jack Straw, John Ball, Geoffrey Lister and William Grindcobbe among them) did more to win the sympathy of later generations for this rising than any careful analysis of what was done by the rebels. Those who had taken up the sword of rebellion died by the avenging sword of retributive justice, and only Richard II's personal inclination towards clemency stood between the people of England and a veritable blood-bath. The Chroniclers are not very reliable on this score, because they were not involved. Important rebel leaders, whose personal responsibility for crimes of violence was not in doubt, were pardoned. The poor found it more difficult to escape. Sober consideration suggests that England as a whole experienced no 'reign of terror' in 1381 and 1382. Indeed, one historian comments, 'Nothing became the English government more than the moderation with which it repressed a revolt it had helped to cause and failed to prevent.'

The Earthquake Synod

After his appointment to the see of Canterbury,

William Courtenay, an avowed enemy of Wycliffe, called a synod at Westminster which opened in May 1382. It was intended to condemn Wycliffe and associate him with the rebellion. 'Let us recognise the malice and iniquity of Master John Wycliffe, both by means of his pestilential doctrines as well as the preaching of his followers and adherents who invariably sowed dissension and provoked the people to rebellion'. The most notorious of his followers named was John Ball, whom they claimed made confession of the influence of Wycliffe before he was executed. No text of this confession survived. The synod assembled on St Dunstan's day (May 19) to condemn Wycliffe and all the Lollards. On that same day, England experienced a violent earthquake, which put fear into the hearts of many at the synod. Courtenay persisted, explaining that the earthquake was sent to purge England of these errors. There were many who feared that Wycliffe's preaching would bring about another rebellion. Oxford could not save him after the recent disturbances and he was thus dismissed from his beloved university and exiled to his parish of Lutterworth for the last two years of his life.

From Lutterworth he appealed to the nation through his English 'tracts'. One, on the *Soldiership of Christ*, explains clearly what he taught about suffering for a just cause. His appeal is certainly not to rebellion, but rather to martyrdom. But his large sympathy with the suffering of the poor did lead him, immediately after the rising was over, to speak of the Peasants' Revolt with moderation and breadth of view. When some of the lords and prelates were thirsting for revenge, he made the proposal that the church property should be given to the secular lords, in order to enable them immediately to relieve the poor of the burdens that had caused the rising.

4. The Translator of the Bible

In one of his more nationalistic moods, John Milton complained that had it not been for the obstinacy of our prelates against the 'divine and admirable spirit of Wycliffe', the names of Huss, Luther and Calvin might never have been known and 'the glory of reforming all our neighbours had been completely ours.' Like many who followed him, Milton detected that Wycliffe had taken the essential steps to bring in the Reformation in England long before Luther set Europe ablaze. Luther was luckier in his friends. The three essential steps towards reformation were:

   to attack the papacy,

   to preach the gospel to the poor,

   to put the people in possession of the word of God.

The Bible played such an essential part in Wycliffe's teaching that the third step could not long be delayed. He was angry with the preaching of his day which spun stories out of half-digested biblical truths. He observed the power of the friar who pretended to know the Bible and put the fear of God into the minds of ignorant people with most unbiblical threats. He was never in doubt that the truths of the Bible should be available to every Christian.

Earlier translation

Parts of the Bible had been translated into English — including the Psalms. The earlier Anglo-Saxon version, which was stll being transcribed in the twelfth century, was of little use. Few knew the language of King Arthur and Saint Dunstan. French Bibles were available to the Norman aristocracy, when they were literate, and Wycliffe spoke with envy of this greater freedom in France.

55

As Wycliffe had challenged the authority of the papacy, already in discredit throughout the land, and had pilloried the hierarchy, he needed to be able to claim more than his own true scholarship as his authority. He clearly found this authority in the Bible, and all his earlier writings show how he depended upon biblical teaching to make his points. It was his desire to base his teaching upon the Bible instead of Catholic tradition. Consequently he was constantly quoting Scripture to confirm his arguments – as for example in the treatise on *Transubstantiation* which caused him so much trouble and led to the break with John of Gaunt. Wycliffe's Bible was the Vulgate and in his Latin writings there was no difficulty about translation. But in his English writings, which were much more widely read, he had to translate the quotations himself or rely upon earlier translations of parts of the Bible.

Wyciffe was a good Latin scholar and a student of the church fathers, but he had neither Hebrew nor Greek. When he translated any passage from the Bible it was from the Vulgate, with careful reference to the use the fathers had made of that passage. There were frequently quotations which did not agree with the Vulgate and he was prepared to give alternative renderings if he felt a doctor of the church had more clearly understood a passage. It is certain that he did not translate all of the version which bears his name, but his disciples did and he inspired an attitude to the Bible as the word of God which made people clamour for the truth.

Resistance to Bible translation

It was to be expected that the priests would resist any attempt to undermine their authority. They told the people what was true and had no desire for them to find out the truth for themselves from the Bible. They complained that by translating the gospel into English, Wycliffe had made it acceptable and more intelligible to 'laymen and even women' than it had been to priests. Wycliffe, they maintained, was casting pearls before swine, contrary to the gospel. He met opposition on every side. He was said to be a heretic, because he spoke the Holy Scripture in English. His opponents asserted the superior authority of the church over the Bible. The church gave the Bible to the world; the Church chose the four Gospels and could have chosen others; the Church sanctions and condemns what she pleases and does not stand under the judgement of the Bible.

Wycliffe's reply was uncompromising: 'Many nations have had the Bible in their own language. The Bible is the faith of the church. Though the Pope and all his clerks should disappear from the face of the earth, our faith would not fail, for it is founded upon Jesus alone, our Master and our God'.

Wycliffe had many supporters, and even in parliament, the rights of Holy Scripture found defenders. John of Gaunt's last word in defence of Wycliffe was in the Upper House in 1390 more than five years after Wycliffe's death, when a motion was being debated to seize all copies of the Bible and destroy them: 'Are we then the very dregs of humanity, that we cannot possess the laws of our religion in our own tongue?'

Effect on Wycliffe

It had already become clear that Wycliffe's undoing was his attack on the Mass, and in particular on the doctrine of transubstantiation. This is a doctrine he had firmly believed up to the year 1378. Put quite simply, it means that when, at the Mass, the 'words of consecration' are pronounced by the priest, the bread and wine are changed into the body and blood of Christ. Three years later, Wycliffe denied this doctrine most vehemently. In fact, he was asserting that there had never been a heresy more cunningly smuggled into the church than transubstantiaton. He denounced it as contrary to Scripture (both Gospels and Epistles), as unsupported by early church tradition, as plainly opposed to the senses, and as based upon false reasoning. He also declared with great vigour that the doctrine was essentially idolatrous and productive of arrogant priestly claims without warrant in Scripture. Wycliffe's language is powerful, as he ridicules the idea that the priest can make God on the altar: 'How canst thou, O priest, who art but a man, make thy Maker? What! the thing that groweth in the fields — that ear which thou pluckest today, shall be God tomorrow! . . . As you cannot make the works that He made, how shall ye make Him who made the works? Woe to the adulterous generation that believeth the testimony of Innocent rather than of the Gospel.'

There was always a strong anti-priestly emphasis in Wycliffe's writings, but this attack on the Mass comes new-minted during the period that he was working on the translaton of the Bible.

The Wycliffe Translation

Archbishop Arundel, writing to the Pope in 1411, puts the matter succinctly: 'This pestilent and wretched John Wyclif of cursed memory, that son of the old serpent . . . endeavoured by every means to attack the very faith and sacred doctrine of Holy Church, devising — to fill up the measure of his malice — the expedient of a new translation of the Scriptures into the mother tongue'.

Put more soberly, we may say that the culmination of the movement for the translation of the Bible into English in the Middle Ages is found in the activities of that group of men who surrounded John Wycliffe, at Oxford and at Lutterworth up to the time of his death in 1384, and who completed after his death the work which he had inspired and initiated. The evidence for Wycliffe's responsibility for the translation is overwhelming, from enemies and friends alike. There are more than 200 copies of parts of the Bible (several New Testament only) scattered throughout the libraries of Britain. Although few contain any evidence of date of copying, they constitute a powerful collection. They all bear a family likeness, despite variations. We can talk with confidence of the *Wycliffe Translation*.

Opposition to the translation continued long after Wycliffe's death. The opposition from the church was based upon several objections. The understanding of Scripture was felt to belong to the priest by virtue of his special grace received when he was ordained. Lay people did not have this grace and a translation would impart to them the views of the translator, rather than the sacred teaching of the church through the Scriptures. The earthly hierarchy was seen as a model of the heavenly, and grace was mediated from above downwards – from the higher clergy to the lower and thence to the laity. Private Bible reading by the laity or uneducated priests who could not read the Vulgate was liable to lead to heresy. There was also a strongly held view that translation was too subtle a task and that the copying of English manuscripts was less well supervised than that of Latin.

These were cumulative arguments, but did not amount to a prohibition. No universal and absolute prohibition of the translation of the Scriptures into the vernacular nor of the use of such translations by the clergy or laity, was so far issued by any council of the church or any pope. Only a few surviving papal letters represent condemnation of translation. One of the most important of these – and one to which Wycliffe is referring when he contrasts the teaching of Innocent with that of the word of God – is that of Innocent III in 1199 on the Waldensian translations. It condemns the users of these, especially those who use them as a basis for preaching, for holding conventicles and setting themselves up against priests of less learning. And although there was no prohibition, those who were responsible for the day-to-day running of the diocese worked on the assumption that possession of vernacular Scriptures was in itself evidence to warrant the suspicion of heresy.

A licence to possess a translation was sometimes granted. One English New Testament in the John Hopkins Library has a note which seems to indicate that it has been approved by two doctors of divinity for use by some lay person. Anne of Bohemia, wife of Richard II, was given such permission. Archbishop Arundel, preaching her funeral oration in 1394, praises her piety and says that he had approved for her use an English version of the four Gospels with glosses upon them. This book was almost certainly a work of the Wycliffites. Such permission to eminent persons was, of course very different from general permission.

The aim of the Wycliffites was undoubtedly to set up a new and all-sufficient authority in opposition to the church. By now the Church was sanctioning much that was unbiblical and Wycliffe was of course opposed to this. He and his followers, therefore, appealed to their regular name for the Bible, 'Goddis lawe' and 'Christis lawe'. But Wycliffe was not only attempting a reform of the church, which might have been accompanied by biblical discussion. He was opening up the authority of the church to the laity. He asserted, and his followers did so even more loudly, that these laws of God were open to the direct understanding of all people on the points most essential to salvation. For such understanding it was necessary that all people should be able to study the Gospels in the tongue in which they might best understand their meaning. This meant removing the tutelage of the church and asserting the liberty of the Christian person.

The beginnings of translation

Wycliffe's attention seems to have been directed to the question of authority in 1374 when he went to Bruges to represent the King and to discuss with representatives of Pope Gregory IX certain payments claimed by him. During the next ten years he was beginning to see the need for an accessible authority in the Bible. Apart from his attention to the theory of civil and ecclesiastical dominion or lordship, to which we hve already referred, his *De Veritate Sacrae Scripturae* (1374) appealed to the Scriptures as of prime authority at this early date. At that time, however, there was no pressure for a translation. Wycliffe was content to argue from the Latin Vulgate. But, ten years later, in the year of Wycliffe's death, translations of the Gospels and Epistles were being copied by a professional scribe. At his trial in 1392, William Smith of Leicester confessed that he had been making these copies since 1384. There is much evidence of continual copying and by 1407 this had reached such a pitch that Archbishop Arundel secured condemnation of this activity along with other aspects of Wycliffe's teaching. This was the first clear prohibition

> 'We resolve therefore and ordain that no one
> henceforth on his own authority translate any
> part of Holy Scripture into the English or any
> other language by way of a book, pamphlet or
> tract, and that no book, pamphlet or tract of
> this kind, whether already recently composed
> in the time of the said John Wyclif or since or
> to be composed in the future, be read in part
> or in whole, publicly or privately, under pain
> of the greater excommunication, until the
> translation shall have been approved by the
> diocesan of the place, or if need be by a
> provincial council'

The prohibition was sternly enforced.

It was at one time thought that John Wycliffe began his translation when he was exiled from Oxford to his parish in Lutterworth in 1382. It now appears that he started work on the translation with the help of many students and colleagues while he was still at Oxford and had access to the patristic commentaries. Somewhere between 1378 and 1382 seems to be the date for the beginning of the translation, and many hands and minds were at work on it. John Wycliffe took the main responsibility, but it is unlikely that the whole New Testament was finished before his death. His followers, who completed the work, were conscious of continuing along lines that he had laid down. From the more than 200 manuscripts still in existence dating from the period 1384 to the prohibition in 1407, including later copies of these, there can be seen to be considerable variations in the text. This is sometimes due to copyists and sometimes to variant versions. There is, however, a basic text that can be called Wycliffe's Bible. There are those who say that this is best read aloud in a Yorkshire accent!

The text

A few examples from Wycliffe's Bible may help to show the power of this translation from the Vulgate and its influence upon later translations. For the purpose of illustration, the spelling has been modernised. From a manuscript in Christ Church, Oxford, we read this rendering of Job 1:6-12:

'On a day, forsooth, when the sons of God were come that they should stand near before God, was nigh among them also Satan. To whom said the Lord, "Whence comest thou?" The which answering said, "I have environed the earth and gone through it." And the Lord said to him, "Whether hast thou not beheld my servant Job, that there be not to him like on earth, a man simple and right and dreading God and going away from evil?" To whom answered Satan, "Whether in vain Job dreadeth God? Whether hast thou not strengthened him and his house and all his substance by everyone? To the works of his hands thou hast blessed, and his possessions wax in the earth; but stretch out thy hand a little, and touch all things that he weldeth, but he curseth thee to thy face''. Then the Lord said to Satan, ''Lo! all things that he hath in thine hand ben; only on him ne stretch thou out thine hand''. And Satan is gone out from the face of the Lord'.

There are slight variations in other manuscripts, but they are usually a matter of tidying up the language and making it clearer.

A manuscript in Corpus Christi College, Oxford, has the following rendering of Isaiah 2: 1-3:

'The word which Isaiah, the son of Amos, saw on Judah and Jerusalem. And in the last days the hill of the house of the Lord shall be made ready in the cap of hills, and shall be raised above little hills, and all heathen men shall flow to him, and many people shall go and shall say, ''Come ye! stay we to the hill of the Lord, and to the house of God of Jacob, and he shall teach us his ways, and we shall go in the paths of him''. Forwhy, the law shall go out of Sion, and the word of the Lord from Jerusalem'.

These two examples show the two main ways in which the translators revised the Vulgate text: the one literal and close to the Latin order of words, the other more free. Wycliffe, in discussion with his followers, had a hand in both forms. The more free version became the popular one, while the Latin-bound version was preferred by the nobles, who possessed copies more for show than use.

A final quote from a manuscript in the British Museum, the Lansdowne manuscript, will show the freedom of style in the popular version. It is a rendering of Acts 28: 1-20:

'And after the third day, he called together the worthiest of the Jews. And when they came he said to them, "Brethren, I did no thing against the people and custom of the fathers, and I was bound at Jerusalem and was taken into the hands of Romans. And when they had asked of me, would have delivered me. But the Jews against saying, I was constrained to appeal to the emperor, not as having any thing to accuse my people. Therefore, for this cause I prayed to see you, and to speak to you. For, for the hope of Israel, I am girt about with this chain'.

It is clear, even from these short extracts, that the English language was emerging from its chains of Anglo-Saxon and Latin. Wycliffe did not have access to the best Greek and Hebrew manuscripts, but he removed the obscurity from the Latin Vulgate and made the Bible sing in the language of the people. The influence of his style upon later generations of Bible translators is considerable and he ranks with Langland and Chaucer in giving a literary form to the English language.

Wycliffe's earliest efforts were concentrated on obtaining a good Latin text and then renderng it as exactly as possible — almost word for word. These versions notably in the Psalms, gave way to a more fluent translation which concentrated on the producton of a readable version, bringing out the full meaning of the original. The work required great scholarship; the range of authorities used is impressive; and great care was taken by Wycliffe to compile a true Latin text, to consult acknowledged experts and to associate with himself a number of other scholars. The connection with the university probably continued after Wycliffe's death. Thus, initiated by Wycliffe and continued by his followers, the Wycliffe Bible presented England with the best translation possible, until a later generation could consult the Greek and Hebrew original.

The use of Wycliffe's Bible

There were, of course, fine copies made for the nobility who at this time were assembling libraries of manuscripts. Many of these remained unused. But there were also smaller and cheaper copies intended for common use among the people. The evidence of later trials shows that many small groups of people were formed for the purpose of reading the Bible together. In this way, even those who were illiterate could hear the Bible read in English. The members of these groups were in danger of prosecution and even death but they continued, and these small and secret Bible readings and meetings proved a fertile breeding ground for the puritanism and non-conformity which has never died out of English religious life.

The Bible that permeated the minds of later generations was not a direct descendent of Wycliffe's Bible. At most a few phrases, particularly from the Psalms, found their way into later translations. Tyndale's return to the original languages meant that versions based upon a Latin translation would soon be out of date.

But in their insistence upon 'Goddis lawe' for everyone and their efforts to present it to the people in an accurate and understandable form, the Wycliffite translators were true precursors of the English Protestant tradition. Until Tyndale's age, the translation inspired by Wycliffe was widely used. Some of the late fourteenth and even early fifteenth century books of devotion contained Bible extracts from Wycliffe. Bishop Reginald Pecock, writing his *Repressor of Over-Much Blaming of the Clergy* (1455) in English, quotes from a later version of Wycliffe, even though he was quite capable of doing his own translations. Murdoch Nisbet turned it into native Scots only a few years before Tyndale's New Testament appeared. It was, however, never printed by the early printers. The commercial risk was too great in view of the prohibitions.

5. The Lollards

Wycliffe was hounded out of Oxford by Archbishop Courtenay, who for years had nourished a hatred of the Reformer and his teaching. In November 1382, Courtenay visited Oxford with the express purpose of condemning Wycliffe. He gathered around him a number of bishops, doctors, priests, students and laymen, and summoned Wycliffe to appear before him. The scholar who had made Oxford his home was weakened by age and long struggles. There was the usual tumult of crowds spoiling for a fight, but when Wycliffe began to speak a silence fell upon all. He commanded immense respect in the university.

Wycliffe said that it was not he who was condemned, but those he called 'the priests of Baal', who disseminated errors in order to sell their Masses. But the decision to expel him was already made and no argument could alter it. Courtenay had obtained permission to banish him to Lutterworth. Wycliffe saw the hopelessness of his case and simply said at last, 'The truth shall prevail!'. Then he left the court with no one daring to stop him.

He withdrew to Lutterworth to live peacefully among his books and his parishioners. The English priests seemed prepared to leave him alone. He could not live long, and it was wrongly assumed that he could do no harm from the country parish of Lutterworth.

But another blow fell when he was summoned to Rome by Pope Urban VI. He did not obey the summons and the reason given was his bodily infirmity. At that time Rome was divided, with half the world recognising Clement VII as Pope and half recognising Urban VI. Urban had too much on his hands to press Wycliffe, and he let the matter drop. But Wycliffe did not. He did not go to Rome, but he confessed his faith to Urban VI.

'I believe that the Gospel of Christ is the whole body of God's law. I believe that Christ, who gave it to us, is very God and very man, and by this it passes all other laws. I believe that the bishop of Rome is bound more than all other men to submit to it, for greatness among Christ's disciples did not consist in worldly dignities or honours, but in the exact following of Christ in his life and manners. No faithful man ought to follow the pope, but in such points as he hath followed Jesus Christ. The pope ought to leave unto the secular power all temporal dominion and rule; and thereunto effectually more and more exhort his whole clergy . . . If I could labour according to my desire in mine own person, I would surely present myself before the bishop of Rome, but the Lord hath otherwise visited me to the contrary, and hath taught me rather to obey God than man'.

Wycliffe's last days

Thus Urban VI had given Wycliffe the opportunity to profess in clear language the principles for which he stood. Wycliffe was not privileged to strike the blow that was eventually struck by Luther, but he prepared the way in England and, through his disciple John Huss, also on the continent. The morning star, but not yet the sun. He was left in peace with his disciples at Lutterworth. Poor Priests went out from that little country town of Lutterworth to spread the gospel and to read the Bible. No one knows how many went, but the people of England were being prepared for a 'Reformation' of their religion which would have a firmly biblical base.

In his last work, the *Trialogus,* Wycliffe wrote allegorically of his last days as being spent in the company of three personages, two of whom were his particular friends and the third his constant adversary: these were *Aletheia, Phronesis* and *Pseudes*. Aletheia (truth) posed questions; Phronesis (understanding) laid down sound doctrine, and Pseudes (falsehood) urged objections.

These three characters carried on a conversation in which great truths were boldly professed. 'The church has fallen', says one of the characters in this work, 'because she has abandoned the gospel, and preferred the laws of the popes'.

These words were the last flicker of the torch. Wycliffe looked upon his end as near. He expected martyrdom – a dungeon in one of the seven hills of Rome or a burning pile in London. 'Why do you talk of seeking the crown of martyrdom afar?', he asked. 'Preach the gospel of Christ to haughty prelates and martyrdom will not fail you. What! I should live and be silent? . . . Never! Let the blow fall, I await its coming'.

But he was spared the blow. He continued tranquilly to preach Jesus Christ; and on 29 December 1384, as he was in his church at Lutterworth, in the midst of his flock, he was suddenly stricken with paralysis. He was carried to his home by affectionate friends and after lingering for two days, he died on the last day of the year.

Lollard triumph

After Wycliffe's death, his disciples gathered fresh courage and England was almost won over to the Reformer's doctrine. These disciples, already called Lollards in Wycliffe's lifetime, recognised a ministry independent of Rome, deriving authority from the word of God alone: 'Every minister can administer the sacrament and attend to the care of souls as well as the pope'. To the licentious wealth of the clergy they opposed a Christian poverty, and to the degenerate asceticism of the mendicant orders, a spiritual and free life. The townsfolk crowded around these humble preachers; the soldiers listened to them, armed with sword and buckler to defend them; the nobility took down the images from their baronial chapels; and even the Royal Family was partly won over to the Reformation.

The walls of St Paul's and other cathedrals were hung with placards aimed at the priests and the friars and their abuses. In 1395, the Lollards petitioned Parliament for a general reform. Their petition is worth quoting: 'The essence of the worship which comes from Rome consists in signs and ceremonies, and not in the effectual ministry of the Holy Ghost: and therefore it is not that which Christ has ordained. Temporal things are distinct from spiritual things: a king and a bishop ought not to be one and the same person'. The things they called upon Parliament to abolish were a mixed lot, including: 'celibacy, transubstantiation, prayers for the dead, offerings to images, auricular confession, war, the arts unnecessary to life, the practice of blessing oil, salt, wax, incense, stones, mitres, and pilgrims' staffs.' The reason given was that 'all these pertain to necromancy and not to theology'.

The King was in Ireland when Pariament was petitioned by the Lollards and Archbishop Arundel, then of York, and Bishop Braybrooke of London, crossed over the Irish Channel to implore the King to do something. Richard II returned to England and forbade Parliament to take the Wycliffite petition into consideration. He then summoned the Lollard lords – Story, Clifford, Latimer and Montacute – and ordered them, on pain of death, to remove any support they were giving to the Lollards.

Almost at once, Richard was overthrown by Bolingbroke – the son of John of Gaunt. The Lollards saw this as the hand of the Lord. The son of their old champion would surely reverse the attitude of the King he had replaced. But the new King, Henry IV, was soon won over by the clergy. Arundel cunningly suggested to Henry that his throne would be insecure if he opposed the church: 'To consolidate your throne, conciliate the clergy, and sacrifice the Lollards', he advised. Henry IV responded and his words were ominous for the survival of the

Lollards: 'I will be the protector of the church'.

Henry IV ascended the throne in the late summer of 1399. By 1401, the infamous act for the burning of heretics, *De Haeretico Comburendo,* was passed by Parliament. The first Lollard martyr was burned in March 1401, eight days before the act became law.

The persecution of the Lollards

Several factors combined to give the Lollards a very ambiguous position. Royal decrees condemned them as heretics and demanded their arrest, but Parliament requested the withdrawal of the ordinance, and so the Lollards would be free for a time. There seems little doubt that they had a considerable support in all classes and that the average Englishman, whether a knight or peasant, shared their dislike of the abuses of the church and its inordinate wealth. On the other hand, England had no consistent experience of dissent. There was only one religion – that of the pope and the bishops. The friars had a great hold over many people through the confessional and there was a persistent belief in the efficacy of the Masses for the dead. But English dislike of excesses came out in the reaction to the Peasants' Revolt and also against those who, contrary to the devotion of Wycliffe himself, treated sacred things lightly. A certain knight of Wiltshire did no good to the Lollard cause when he ran out of the church with the host and locked himself in to eat it with his dinner. The church, though disliked, was in a strong position. The Lollards' influence spread for a while, but eventually the people could not prevent the church from persecuting them.

The spread of the Lollards out from Lutterworth after Wycliffe's death was phenomenal, and for the church alarming. The first to make any considerable impression on the people of Leicester was a priest named William Swynderby. He was already known locally for his prophetic denunciation of the wives of Leicester for their gaiety, before he joined Wycliffe's followers. He had also adopted the life of a hermit before joining with a group of these followers to live in a little deserted chapel outside the walls of the city. No one interfered with them and they encouraged one another in their opinions and debated the new doctrines. Swynderby preached for miles around in all the neighbouring towns of Leicestershire, but had his greatest following in Leicester itself. The Bishop of Lincoln forbade him to preach in sacred ground after his successes in some of the largest churches, so he retired to a mill and preached there. Enormous crowds came out to hear him. He denounced the clergy, using Wycliffe's arguments against the wealth of the prelates and unjust excommunication; he called on the people to withhold their tithes from wicked churchmen, and exhorted husbands and fathers to beware of the priest's intimacy with their families. But he taught no revolution or anything subversive of public order.

In July 1382, when Wycliffe was being expelled from Oxford, Swynderby was arrested. The friars, jealous of his success, brought exaggerated charges of heresy against him. The mayor and some leading citizens of Leicester came to his defence, declaring that the charges were false, but it was to no avail. He was condemned to the stake. At the last moment, John of Gaunt, who happened to be in Lincoln where the trial had taken place, intervened and he was spared. By recanting all his imputed heresies Swynderby obtained his freedom. This surrender did him so much harm in the eyes of his followers that he had to move elsewhere. He preached at Coventry for nearly a year and made many converts, until the clergy forced him to move to the west country.

Swynderby's work at Leicester was continued by his friends and by fresh helpers from Oxford. John Aston travelled through England, staff in hand, and visited the 'deserted chapel' where Swynderby had lived with Wycliffe's followers. The chapel was soon referred to as the Lollard Chapel. John Aston on this flying visit to

Leicester preached against transubstantiation, a thing which Swynderby had never dared to do. Wycliffe's position was what is called 'consubstantiation'. He venerated the host, but did not worship it; the bread and wine remained bread and wine, but Christ was truly present. This became the doctrine of the Lollards although some extreme attacks upon transubstantiation led to wild statements that were far from Wycliffe's position.

The first Lollard martyrdom was that of William Sawtre, a pious priest who declared that instead of adoring the cross, he adored the Christ on the cross. Wycliffe would have approved. This was not heresy, but devotion. It was seen, however, as an attack upon the profitable relics of the church. Sawtre was dragged to St Paul's; his hair was shaved off; a layman's cap was placed on his head; and the primate handed him over to the 'mercy' of the Earl Marshal of England. He was burnt alive at Smithfield.

Once started, the persecution could not be stopped. The clergy had tasted blood. They drew up the articles known as the 'Constitutions of Arundel' which forbade the translation and reading of the Bible without the permission of the Ordinary (i.e. a bishop or other high officer of the church), and styled the pope, 'not a mere man, but a true God'. What was called the Lollards' Tower in the Archbishop's palace in Lambeth was soon filled with followers of Wycliffe. Many of them carved on the walls their sorrow and their hopes.

After the merciless pursuit of the 'Poor Priests' and the humbler of Wycliffe's followers, the church attacked the so-called Lollard lords. One outstanding figure who was cruelly hounded to his death was Sir John Oldcastle, later Lord Cobham, who had many of Wycliffe's writings copied and stored at his place in Cowling. His home became a centre for Lollards and he was marked out for destruction. Henry IV protected him while he lived, but his son Henry V allowed priests to have their way, and he was executed in 1417.

The Lollards were driven to hide themselves in the humblest ranks of society, cut off from learning and edifying conversation. They were forced into ignorance, and many were cut off also from the source of their understanding in the works of Wycliffe. There was little educated or high ranking support, for the church had successfully cut down their leadership. And so they became plain, meek and often timid folk, attracted by the word of God, aware of the unscriptural errors in current church practice, but powerless, except to prepare for the coming Reformation when England would be ready for the truth.

The Lollards' humble piety, their passive resistance, the shameful treatment which they bore with resignation, betrayed the pride of the priests, and stirred the most generous hearts and minds to doubts and vague desires. For a time, especially under Henry V, efforts were made to silence those doubts and quench the vague desires. The Middle Ages were temporarily restored. But it was a hopeless task. The morning star had shown the possibility of light and the dawn could not be held back.

6. Wycliffe, Huss, Luther

It has been generally assumed that John Huss was a disciple of John Wycliffe and that he simply took the master's teaching to his native Prague and imitated the English movement there. That is far too narrow an interpretation of the events, and pays too little attention to the immense amount of work done in Czechoslovakia on the origins of the Reformation among the Czechs.

John Huss was powerfully influenced by Wycliffe as we shall see, and in fact he was eventually condemned to death for Wycliffite doctrines. But a parallel movement to that developed by Wycliffe in Oxford evolved in Prague. The Czech movement too began in the university.

The native Czech Reformation movement

Dating from the middle of the fourteenth century, two reform movements shook the church: the one we have followed with Wycliffe in Oxford, the other in Bohemia. At first they had little contact with each other and only later merged when the mind of John Huss was tuned to that of the older John Wycliffe.

The major figure in the early Bohemian movement was the Austrian Conrad Waldhausen, but to his name must be added the Czech theologians Milič of Kromeriz, Matthew of Janov and Peter of Chelciče. It was Matthew who, like Wycliffe, identified the movement with the university circle. He was a celebrated scholar, a master of the university of Paris, whose own chief work, *Regulae Veteris et Novi Testamenti* (Rules of the Old and New Testaments) was thoroughly imbued with biblical principles in the spirit of the reform movement.

John Huss joined himself enthusiastically to this reform movement in Bohemia, and when in 1402 he was appointed as preacher to the Bethlehem Chapel in Prague, he became its chief spokesman. At that time, Huss was already an ardent adherent to Wycliffe's philosophical realism. As this adherence was well known and the Bethlehem Chapel was in the gift of the university, we may assume that Wycliffe had his sympathisers at least among the doctors of the university. But at this stage nothing was known of Wycliffe's theological writings. When these were brought into the country by Jerome of Prague, John Hass read them eagerly. He found in them many ideas that were similar to, or even identical with, those of the native reformers. We have to remember that Marsiglio of Padua and William of Ockham had been read by educated men all over Europe. The revolutionary thought of these two outstanding scholars and the seminal ideas which they spread were the common stock of every university and the basis from which effective reform took place. All the reform movements were interdependent in this sense. If Huss was dependent upon Wycliffe, the English Reformer was himself dependent upon a host of others, such as Grosseteste, John of Paris, Marsiglio and Ockham.

But beside this common pool of ideas, the various national movements possessed their individual traits and differences. For example, the Czech reformers like Milič and Matthew had no such faith in state support as Wycliffe had. The older Czech reformers placed their chief reliance upon the cultivation of the spiritual life, renunciation of the world, the austerities of apostolic poverty, frequent Communion and the 'imitation of Christ'. Matthew of Janov had no faith in the role of clergy. He believed the needed reform would come from the common people. The younger generation of Czech reformers, including Huss, advocated a moderate role for the state in the reform of the church. In this the influence of Wycliffe was clearly apparent.

The struggle against Wycliffism in Prague

The outburst in 1403 in the University of Prague against the teaching of John Wycliffe was mainly over his philosophy. Theological elements were added because it was much easier to secure condemnation on theological than on philosophical grounds. The first attack was made not against Huss, but against the senior Czech member of the theological faculty, Stanislav of Znojmo. A few years later in 1408, Stephen of Páleč was also attacked. Both were summoned to Rome and imprisoned en route at Bologna. They were freed by Pope Alexander V but were compelled to recant their Wycliffism. Returning to Prague they became the bitterest opponents of any Wycliffite tendency in the reform movement. This defection by the two senior men forced the 37-year-old John Huss into the forefront of the Wycliffite party. He was, of course, involved before but now he became the acknowledged leader. The choice was an obvious one because he was the ablest among the young theologians.

John Huss on 'Simony'

Wycliffe's book *De Simonia* was among the books brought to Prague by Jerome from Oxford. Huss read the book and was soon involved in controversy. In January 1404, Johann Hübner deliberately provoked the controversy by asserting that Wycliffe was a heretic and those who read his books were sharing in his heresy. Huss replied by accusing Hübner of falsifying Wycliffe's teaching. But he centred his defence on *Simony*. He quoted Hübner as saying that 'the supreme pontiff should simply be obeyed and we should reprove him in nothing'. This doctrine was fervently denied by John Huss: 'You speak contrary to the canons, and are therefore a heretic if you assertively and pertinaciously hold to it'. It was at this point that he quoted from Wycliffe's newly arrived book *De Simonia,* regarding the three kinds of heresies: apostasy, blasphemy and simony.

Huss was not the only person to attack that all-pervading vice of the church of his day. It had been the target for all the advocates of reform during that dark period of the 'Babylonian captivity' of the papacy in Avignon. Matthew of Cracow about this time also published his *squalores curiae Romanae,* in which he reached the radical conclusion that since the court of Pope Boniface IX was the very source of this vice, any contact with it was in itself reprehensible. There were others, including the rector of the University of Cracow, who had attacked simony. It would appear that many of the universities of Europe were horrified at the goings on at the papal court in Avignon. The views of Wycliffe at Oxford was no surprise, nor was his a lonely voice. His eloquence and scholarship, however, gave courage to others and there is little doubt that John Huss was inspired by, if not dependent entirely upon, Wycliffe. He was at this time acquainted with only a few of Wycliffe's works, but his own writing on simony carried Wycliffe's ideas further than the book he had read. Huss was an independent thinker who admired Wycliffe and eagerly sought more of his works.

The condemnation of John Huss

In 1407 two young Czech students visited Oxford and returned with a number of Wycliffe's books, including *De Veritate Sacrae Scripturae* (On the Truth of the Holy Scriptures), *De Domino Divine* (On Divine Lordship), *De Ecclesia* (On the Church), and perhaps *De Potestate Papae* (On the Power of the Pope). When John Huss studied these and listened to reports of what Wycliffe was teaching, he realised that fundamentally he was at one with the English reformer, although their views were not identical.

John Huss was well aware of the danger he courted, both by supporting Wycliffe and attacking the abuses of the church. In his books on simony, published in 1413, he makes this quite clear. He was not deliberately being polemical, but, as he says, writing 'not that good men be defamed and harmed, but that they should guard themselves against evil, and that evil men should repent'. He leaves no doubt about the danger he puts himself in by doing this:

> 'I have written these books, knowing that I shall receive for it neither praise, favour nor material profit from the avaricious priests and worldly people. For I do not desire these things from them, but a reward from God and their salvation. If I receive denunciation and persecution, I have decided that it is better to suffer death for the truth than to receive material reward for flattery'.

The first conflict came early, and began with disputes over the authority of the Pope. In this Huss had the support of King Wenceslas. It was a bitter, personal struggle between the young Archbishop Zbyněk and the rising young preacher of the Bethlehem Chapel who was soon to become rector of the university, John Huss. When the Council of Pisa deposed and excommunicated the two rival popes, Gregory and Benedict in 1409, the German element in the University of Prague (including Archbishop Zbyněk) remained faithful to Gregory; the Czech masters strongly supported King Wenceslas' policy of neutrality. It was this event that brought about the split between Huss and Zbyněk.

The Archbishop had earlier ordered the surrender of all Wycliffe's writings, philosophical or theological. Huss obeyed under protest, others refused. The Archbishop then used his authority against the reform movement (largely because it was Czech), on the grounds that they preached Wycliffe doctrine − even after Wycliffe had been condemned. The question of the popes was resolved. Zbyněk accepted the authority of Pope Alexander, but smarted under the humiliation and became even more opposed to the Czechs and to Huss in particular. Changes in the constitution of the university had put the Czechs in command and Huss was appointed rector in 1409. A personal animosity arose and Zbyněk became more and more determined to punish 'the insolent Czech'. He sent a delegation to the papal court, now that he had surrendered, asking for support against Huss, whom he portrayed as a Wycliffite heretic.

The Pope, wishing to please his new disciple empowered the Archbishop to proceed against Wycliffe's influence in Bohemia and Moravia by forbidding preaching in all but parochial and monastic churches. This was specifically aimed against the Bethlehem Chapel. This angered John Huss because preaching was his main method of communicating the gospel, and he refused to be silenced. To obey the order and be silent in the face of a misrepresentation of Wycliffe would be to betray his deepest convictions. Pope Alexander died and Huss appealed to the new Pope John XXIII. The Archbishop excommunicated Huss, but he continued to preach and ignored the excommunication.

After Zbyněk's death the archiepiscopal party continued their hostillity, but did not dare attack Huss while he had the King's support. They needed the King's permission to sell indulgences for the Pope's war. This sale of indulgences was one of the main points of dispute between the Reformers and the papal party. Huss was now in real danger. His friends counselled him not to attack the sale of indulgences, because that might cost him the King's support. They were right. Huss felt he had to stand against what he called 'trafficking in holy things' and he lost the King's support. When in June 1412 he denounced the papal bull urging the sale of indulgences, and called the Pope 'Antichrist', he lost the support of many of his friends and of King Wenceslas. His opponents not only insisted upon the closing of the Bethlehem Chapel, but attempted to raze it to the ground. The Czechs prevented its destruction, but could not save John Huss.

In October 1412, Huss left the country and sought protection in the castle of one of his noble friends. Like Luther after him, he used this time of exile to write. The exile lasted about a year and a half, during which most of his Czech writings were produced. As he could no longer preach from the pulpit of his beloved Bethlehem Chapel, he poured out his proclamations in writing. The most important of these vernacular writings was *An Exposition of the Faith,* which was supplemented with *An Exposition of the Decalogue* and *An Exposition of the Lord's Prayer.* These were intended to teach the common people what to believe, what to do and how to pray. He also prepared for popular reading a selection of his sermons. His sharply polemical books *On Simony* were also written at this time. His writings were heavily dependent upon Scripture and those fathers of the church who were most biblical in their approach. One of his favourites was Saint Gregory. One Latin writing also comes from this period, *De Ecclesia* (On the Church).

With the Christian world divided in its allegiance to three popes, a council was held in Constance, from 1414 to 1418. After three years of examining the claims of Gregory, Benedict and John, the council eventually proclaimed Martin V Pope in 1418. The council had also, at an early stage, condemned Wycliffe as a heretic and revolutionary.

It was to that council that John Huss was summoned. He was given safe conduct by the Hungarian king Sigismund (brother to king Wenceslas) but was found guilty of heresy and, when he refused to recant his views, was burnt at the stake, outside the city wall, on 6 July 1415.

Martin Luther and John Huss

Although John Wycliffe was the unchallenged 'morning star of the Reformation' in England, where all later reformers looked back to him for inspiration, John Huss was more directly influential than Wycliffe in Europe. Luther makes more than one reference to him and the crime of his burning. In his *Pagan Servitude of the Church* Luther writes: 'Councils have often erred, especially that at Constance, which was the most wicked of them all'; and more specifically in *An Appeal to the Ruling Classes*: 'Sigismund, the religious-minded emperor, had no success after the Council of Constance, when he allowed those rogues to break the safe-conduct which had been given to John Huss.' And although Luther is not concerned in that treatise to support the teaching of John Huss, he is prepared to go so far as to say, 'to my way of thinking he wrote nothing erroneous'. He repeats with passion, 'John Huss was unjustly banned and he was burned contrary to God's will'.

It was Luther who instigated the publication of two large folio volumes of Huss's chief works. Thus Wycliffe's works were preserved in Prague when they were destroyed in England and his ideas perpetuated through the reissuing of Huss's chief works.

The influence of John Huss on the Reformation was considerable. Luther may have thought little of the Hussite theology, and he would have had some difficulty with John Wycliffe's views on transubstantiation, but it was the Lollards in England and the Hussites in Bohemia who prepared the ground to receive his word when the time came for it to be spoken.

The Englishness of the English Reformation

While there is little doubt that Wycliffe influenced John Huss considerably and that Luther learnt much (including Wycliffite tendencies) from John Huss, it is not possible to see a smoothly evolving development. What happened in England was neither a preparation for a continental Reformation nor an echo of it. Luther influenced the later stages of the English Reformation, but he did not make it.

There was a unique Englishness about the English Reformation which goes back to Wycliffe. He was responsible for English religious thought advancing on a three-pronged front: patriotism, rationalism and evangelical holiness. He was a *patriot,* or so he styled himself, in that his anti-papal assumptions were based upon a conviction that the pope's authority did not apply in England. He was an apostle of *evangelical holiness* in that he (and, even more, his followers the Lollards) protested violently against clerical laxities and a tendency throughout the hierarchy to lower standards of morality and devotion. And to these characteristic notes, heard in all the medieval Reformers, he added a third note, that the *individual* has a right to direct access to the fountain head of doctrine. To this end he put the Bible into English.

Wycliffe's linking of proper 'lordship' with merit, by which teaching power is entrusted only into competent hands; his evangelical doctrine of the atonement and of personal salvation; his doctrine of the church as the 'Communion of Saints', and his attack on transubstantiation are all the result of a fusion in his mind of those three elements — patriotism, rationalism and holiness.

7. The Radical Reformation and the Anabaptists

When the full force of the Reformation broke forth in the fifteenth and sixteenth centuries it issued in three recognisable streams of churchmanship: Lutheran, Calvinist and Anglican. There were considerable differences in these three and on the whole they remained distinct. But, increasingly, it is now recognised that there was a fourth stream. It is sometimes referred to as the Radical Reformation and it is this stream which Wycliffe influenced most profoundly.

There is less uniformity in this fourth stream than in any of the other three. Angel M Mergal and George Williams have produced for *The Library of Christian Classics* a volume of documents illustrative of the Radical Reformation. The first part of the volume deals with what is sometimes called 'the left wing of the Reformation' and the second with Evangelical Catholicism. In the first part, George Williams attempts to classify the great variety of material into three groups. Each of these groups owes much to Wycliffe and each, while flourishing in the sixteenth century, continued to inform the religious life of Europe and particularly England.

The three groups are the *Anabaptists,* the *Spiritualists* and the *Evangelical Rationalists.* All three were dissatisfied by the way the Reformation developed into territorial churches which began to show the same rigidity as Rome. Common to writers in all three groups is a distinctive Christology, insisting on the celestial rather than natural, origin of the flesh of Christ, and a correspondingly mystical-physical view of the Lord's Supper. Common also to them all was an acceptance of the freedom of the will in the striving for sanctification. But most evident of all was their common resistance to the linking of church and state. They would not tolerate the trespassing of pope, town council, prince or king upon the rights of the loyal subjects of the King of Kings.

The established and protected churches, whether Protestant or Catholic, were eventually forced to compromise with the state in order to prevent the separation of citizenship and membership of the church. The proponents of the Radical Reformation, on the other hand, had learnt to look back to the church of the New Testament or to the early fathers, and strove to restore the early purity of the church. Most of them thus abandoned any hope of a Christian society conterminous with political boundaries, except at the end of time.

In most of the countries of Europe, the Radical Reformation was ruthlessly suppressed both by Catholics and Protestants. Luther, Zwingli and Calvin set the pattern for suppression of these dissenting elements which had taken the teaching of the early reformers to their logical conclusion.

Within the Radical Reformation, there was sharp division between those who (like the Anabaptists) looked back to the days of the church of the New Testament and the early martyrs, and those who (like the Spiritualists) looked firmly forward to the church that was to be. There is no doubt that in this division the influence of Wycliffe was most strongly seen among the Anabaptists. The Bible was the measure of what he regarded as the true church. But this is the only sense in which the Anabaptists would have found Wycliffe sympathetic to their views. He would not have approved their irresponsibility with regard to the state. Those successors of the Anabaptists who developed on quite different lines in England were consciously influenced by Wycliffe, or rather by the Lollards. The English Baptists were very much more involved with the state.

The effect of printing

Although the early printers did not print Wycliffe's Bible, and his books had been destroyed in England, not to emerge again until the nineteenth century, the advent of printing helped to emphasize his teaching. Books and even more, pamphlets, became part of the landscape. How Wycliffe would have loved that! His books did not come off the printing presses, but his ideas did. His way of thinking and communicating became the normal way. Printing led to an antipathy to visual images; a new literalism in the interpretation of the Scriptures; a new cult of the 'simple', meaning that which was openly intelligible rather than mystical; an insistence on the right of ordinary people to understand the words and actions of the priest, and to work out their own religion. This meant a vernacular Bible, and soon a better Bible than Wycliffe's became available in England.

A new form of argued theology arose, which reached a high point in Calvin, but was in the air generally. Wycliffe would have been ready for this and had prepared England for it. The medieval church, still clinging to power all over Europe, was unprepared. There arose in people of the printing age a suspicion of human authority, a suspicion of anything which cannot be put down in black and white, a tendency to emphasise local nationalisms with national languages, a retreat from universal languages like Latin. There was a strong movement towards personal religion and holiness, away from the institutional. The picture of English dissent in the seventeenth century looks like the result of adding Wycliffe's theology to the social temper of the Peasants' Revolt.

Revolutionary Anabaptists

When Baptists have hesitated to be associated with the *Anabaptists* of the continent it has usually been because of the confusion between the three different kinds that emerged. These can be called *Revolutionary, Contemplative* and *Evangelical* Anabaptists.

All Anabaptists stressed the recovery or restoration of the church of the past, but the Revolutionary Anabaptists regarded the Old Testament as well as the New as normative for the theology and constitution of the church. Although Wycliffe treats the whole Bible, Old and New Testament, as holy writ, he looks only to the New Testament as the model for the church. In fact, his writings on the Scriptures are overwhelmingly on the New Testament. Even when he does deal with the Old Testament, it is interpreted through the New. But the Revolutionary Anabaptists, when they set up their New Commonwealth communities in Münster, Amsterdam and elsewhere, drew more and more on the Old Testament in the regulation of their society. This led to the establishment of fierce, and sometimes polygamous, theocracies.

It is not difficult to see how Wycliffe's teaching could be exaggerated to lead to this conclusion, but he would never have approved this use of the Bible. The opponents of biblical translation were encouraged in their opposition by such behaviour, and it was such abuse of his teachings that led his opponents to accuse Wycliffe of causing and even supporting the Peasants' Revolt.

Contemplative Anabaptists

These are the furthest removed from the Revolutionary Anabaptists. John Denek, who had connections with all trends in the Radical Reformation, is a good example of a Contemplative Anabaptist. He followed the example of Jesus in submitting to baptism (rebaptism) in his maturer years, administered the rite to new converts, and accepted the instruction of Jesus in every point. He felt most deeply the claim of the inner Christ. The words of Wycliffe in his sermon *On the Perfect Life* would be gladly accepted by him: 'Christ, not compelling, but freely counselling each man to perfect life, saith thus, If any man will come after me let him deny himself, and take his cross and follow me. Then let us forsake ourselves, such as we have made us in doing sin, and dwell we such as we are made by grace'.

John Denek identified this inner Christ with the inner Word common to all mankind wherever, 'as though a spark blown upon by the Spirit, it bursts into the flame of conscience.'

Evangelical Anabaptists

These have certain traits in common with the Revolutionary Anabaptists, but for them only the New Testament was prescriptive for doctrine, ethics and policy. And basically this was also Wycliffe's view. The Old Testament and its Apocrypha were interpreted allegorically or typically, which was more or less Luther's way too.

They were distrustful of doctrines centring on the Holy Spirit. The historic Jesus — his specific instructions, his life, and his crucifixion — was for them normative. They understood that the imitation of Christ, from hazardous rebaptism in some Germanic Jordan to a possible martyr's pyre, represented the fulness of the Christian Way.

Among the Hutterite Anabaptists of Moravia, the impulse towards community developed into a highly disciplined communism of production as well as of consumption. Church and community became one, and the gospel became a new law. While their discipleship was in danger of degenerating into legalism, they refused to intellectualise their faith and produced no systematic theology.

Spiritualists

We must disabuse our mind of the modern sense of this word. For this group spirit was central in their lives and thinking: their driving force was the enlightening or rational spirit. They knew that the spirits had to be tested, but they were always confident that the source of their authority was none other than the Holy Spirit. Moreover, they taught that the Holy Spirit was the inspiration of the

Holy Scripture, of the prophets of old and of the present day, and he was also the cohesive power of Christian fellowship. He was superior to the Holy Scripture, the clergy and the church.

There are three groupings of spiritualists, as with the Anabaptists. The Revolutionary Spiritualists were charismatic, experiencing the driving power of the spirit; the Rational Spiritualists were speculative, grounded more in the inner spirit than in the Holy Spirit; the Evangelical Spiritualists were more mystical than speculative, nurtured by the Johannine writings – Gospel and Epistles.

Briefly, Evangelical Spiritualism is by nature individualistic, while the establishment of a holy commonwealth is often the goal of Revolutionary Spiritualism, which draws upon the prophetic visions of corporate salvation. The goal of Rational Spiritualism is peace, the ordering of the disparate intellectual patterns in religion to achieve harmony. Rational and Evangelical Spiritualism are tolerant and accomodating because of their individualism, whereas Revolutionary Spiritualism is righteously indignant in its collective intolerance as it pushes forward to a disciplined theocratic community.

The children of the Reformation seem often to be caught between anger at abuses in the unreformed church and the desire for peaceful change. Wycliffe's anger at the friars is about as inflammatory as any writing by revolutionary radicaks! In England the two tendencies are well illustrated in the involvement of Puritans in the Civil War of the seventeenth century and the traditional pacifist attitude of the Quakers.

The Evangelical Rationalists

The third subdivision of the Radical Reformation represents the spirit of reform and was at its strongest in France, Spain and countries of southern Europe. Many did not break away from the Catholic Church but sought radical reform from within. Erasmus, with his strong support of Martin Luther, is a puzzle to Protestants. There is little doubt that he is a reformer and much of his teaching goes further than Luther in this respect. Apart from Erasmus, there is Lefèvres of France and Juan de Valdès of Spain. These men had much in common with that small band of free spirits who broke away from the Roman church: Servetus, condemned by Rome and Geneva; Bernardino Ochino, Sebastian Castello, George Biandrata, and the notorious Faustus Socinus, whose name formed an abusive adjective, 'Socinian' used by orthodox Christians for many years.

Common to all these, whether they remained within the Catholic Church or were condemned by Protestant and Catholic alike, was a recognition of the place of natural piety and of both intuitive and speculative reason alongside that of Scripture. In the Unitarians and in the Socinians of Poland, this subgroup of the Radical Reformation found institutional expression. Like the Anabaptists, they strove to create disciplined congregations on the New Testament pattern. Like the Spiritualists, they strove to carry through the Reformation impulse into the realm of theology, church order and the sacraments.

The Radical Reformation in England and America

The Radical Reformation was ruthlessly suppressed on the continent of Europe. This did not happen to the same extent in England or subsequently in America. The reason may be due to the early influence of Wycliffe, who prepared the way for a Reformation which never saw the violent upheavals experienced by Germany and other parts of Europe in the destructive conflict between Reformation and Counter-Reformation.

When Bonhoeffer described religion in America as 'Protestantism without Reformation', he viewed it critically, as a German Lutheran must. But what he did not say was that it was also Protestantism without

Counter-Reformation. America's church situation is also the result of historical peculiarities in English history. While in Europe the Reformation of the territorial churches coincided and clashed with the Radical Reformation, in England the two phases were spaced a century apart. These two phases were the national Reformation under the king in the sixteenth century and the social Reformation under Cromwell in the seventeenth century.

In England, unlike Germany, the voices of dissent were able to make a permanent contribution to the structuring of a pluralistic society. This is seen in the differences between the German or Dutch Anabaptists and the English Baptists. The latter fought for the principle of separation of church and state, but they were as interested in the strengthening of the state as they were in the purification of the church. The Puritans and even the Separatists among them were able to participate directly in the formation of an open and responsible democracy, in a way that was never possible for the even more heroic and ethically resolute Anabaptists of sixteenth century Germany.

Wycliffe's part in the three historic events of the English Reformation

It is difficult not to see the figure of John Wycliffe looming above the three great historic events which made English Protestantism and English political reform what it is. The Peasants' Revolt of 1381; the official break with Rome in the Reformation Parliament called in 1529; the Civil War in 1649; all three are linked to Wycliffe.

Wycliffe gave voice and authoritative word to the grievances that led to the Peasants' Revolt. His disapproval was confined to the disorderly way in which the wrongs were to be righted. In fact, they were not righted, for reasons that he could have foretold. He saw that rights gained in such a way would be lost in the subse quent suppression — and they were. But his comments on the Revolt were moderate, with an underlying sympathy for the cause.

When Henry VIII broke with Rome and proclaimed that he was to be recognised as the supreme earthly authority in the church of England, he was following a pattern laid down by Wycliffe. And Wycliffe had also seen that the king would have to carry the people with him. Henry was careful to call his Parliament in 1529, after the fall of Wolsey, for this very purpose. The Parliament, destined to be the great 'Reformation Parliament' of England, remained in session until 1536. This was an unprecedented duration for such a body. Parliament was the only means open to Henry of trying to present a national front to the hostile and sometimes very critical outside world. At the same time it commended his proceedings to the nation. This was Wycliffe's model: a church in England, free from the illegitimate lordship of Rome, presided over by the king, with the approval of the nation. Wycliffe would have seen the King as a reformer — rejecting payments to Rome, bringing England into line with France and Germany in its possession of the Bible in its own language, purging the clergy and the monasteries of their wealth. Although his divorce from Catherine of Aragon may have been Henry's motive for the break with Rome, what he set in motion was Wycliffe's Reformation.

When the Civil War came to an end on 30 January 1649, a transformation had taken place in England. The attempt by Charles I to reimpose a medieval church, and the just complaints that accompanied the protest against his absolute rule, were in a different world from Wycliffe's and it is hard to imagine his role in the conflict. The unjust treatment of the poor, the limited rights of appeal against the royal decisions and judgements, would have found him on the side of the poor. He would have preached the rights of the individual. But the overthrow of a legitimate monarch would have been beyond his compass. However, he had influenced the genius behind the rebellion more than any other thinker. Cromwell's guiding principle was the new Protestantism in a fiercely concentrated form. Debating with the army leaders in 1647, he called for and expected biblical exposition and prayer at every session, he looked for biblical references as each point was made. And when it came to his attitude to personal power, he agonised over his Bible to find where the right path lay. Wycliffe would have understood and approved that attitude to the Bible.

8.   The political implications of the Civil War

The implications of Wycliffe's teaching on 'lordship' and his insistence upon universal direct access to the word of God could not be worked out fully in his own generation. The political structures were too deeply entrenched to be overthrown by the concept of 'lordship by grace alone' or by the judgement of the word of God.

But in his own lifetime there were those who preached the right of all to justice and the unlawful holding of property by an immoral church. The Peasants' Revolt was an untidy political attempt to assert these truths. When it came to the point, the King's authority was not challenged nor made subject to higher law. Kings had been deposed or murdered before, and Richard himself was eventually deposed by Bolingbroke. But while any man was king the people accepted his authority and were prepared to believe that an appeal to him would be heard. There were, of course, exceptions. Yet 1381 was too early to press home the logic of Wycliffe's views of the rights of man and the authority of the Bible over church and state.

Wycliffe's ideas did not die, but grew. Printing disseminated them and gave them greater authority. England's Reformation in the sixteenth century was led by the King and it involved putting into practice some of what Wycliffe taught – the denial of the authority of Rome over England, the availability of the Bible in the English language, the worship of God in the vernacular, the reform of the clergy and the curtailing of the power of the friars and the monasteries. The Prayer Books put into the hands of the people explanatations and details of the services of the church, no longer, as Wycliffe had complained, kept as mysteries in the hands of the priests. The doctrine of transubstantiation was denounced and the host was venerated, but not worshipped. Later in the sixteenth century Queen Elizabeth made more concessions to construct a Church of England, but once having made those concessions she insisted upon obedience like any pope. Persecution of Catholics and, under Mary, of Protestants, left a stain on the development of English religious life, although many of the persecutions were as much political as religious. But at the start of the seventeenth century James I ordered an official translation of the Bible, without note or comment. Wycliffe could not have wished for anything more triumphant than the Authorised Version of the Bible in 1611.

The political elements in Wycliffe's teaching

Wycliffe's theory of 'divine lordship' meant that all authority rested on God and that, while a spark of that lordship might be given to man, God still held control. If the owner was not 'in grace' his ownership was invalid. Wycliffe applied this particularly to the church which was the wealthiest landowner of the day. But he did not hesitate to apply it also to the secular lords. The logical conclusion was that it should apply equally to the king. The usual way of applying that judgement was to attack the king's advisers. The king himself was sacrosanct except to those who schemed to replace him.

Wycliffe lived through a period in which Edward III passed into senility with an immense reputation; the Black Prince, his putative successor, wasted away with illness; the boy King Richard triumphed and declined until he was deposed. While Wycliffe did not apply his doctrine of lordship to the king, he must often have considered it.

The support of Henry IV was dependent less upon obedience to God's law than upon currying favour with the church. His son Henry V went further in this direction. The Wars of the Roses presented a spectacle which could hardly have improved the status of the monarchy as 'lord by the grace of God.' Henry VII was welcomed as stabilising the throne, and Henry VIII carried the nation with him when they broke from Rome. Queen Elizabeth gave England her period of glory and she was forgiven much. James I carefully went along with the popular view – retaining the Protestant faith independent of Rome, authorising the English Bible and suppressing the traitorous acts of Roman Catholics. His son believed in the divine right of kings, but had less understanding of the people.

The main issue of the Civil War was whether the rights of the king could be challenged by the people. Thomas Helwys had already in James's reign incurred the wrath that sent him to Newgate, because in his book *The Mystery of Iniquity* he had dared to say that 'the king is a mortal man', and to teach that while he has power over the body of his subjects, he has no power over their souls. Helwys pleaded for freedom to worship God in a way consonant with conscience. Charles I accepted Wycliffe's position that all power was from God. The responsibility of the king to hold power under God was never more clearly expressed than by Charles himself: 'We have no other intention but by our government to honour Him, by Whom Kings reign and to procure the good of our people, and for this end to preserve the right and authority wherewith God has vested us'. But for Charles there was no other judge than God. The struggle with the Parliamentarians was over the right of others to judge and advise the king. What was the authority of Parliament?

Wycliffe's opponent was never the king, although had he lived in the following century, he might well have opposed Henry V in his defence of the clergy against the Lollards. His main opponent was the church, and that was personified in the person of the pope. When Richard II called his first Parliament, he asked Wycliffe to answer the question, whether the king could withhold the treasures of the realm for its defence, even when they were demanded by the pope. A careful study of Wycliffe's answer leaves no doubt as to where he would have stood in the seventeenth century battle between King and Parliament. He might well have disapproved of much that was done and how it was done, but his teaching leads directly to Cromwell and Pym. Cromwell agonising with the Bible in prayer was a disciple of Wycliffe. But he went beyond Wycliffe in putting that teaching into political form. For there is no doubt at all that Wycliffe would not have approved of the execution of the King.

English religious Dissent

As early as 1567, there is evidence of a separatist meeting being visited by the sheriffs of the City of London and called to account for illegal assembly. This was in Plumbers' Hall and representatives of this congregation, with their minister, spent the night in the cells. The next morning they were charged before the Lord Mayor of London. Congregational and Baptist groups had a precarious existence until the Civil War, and many of them were willing recruits to Cromwell's Model Army. Once Dissent felt it had the Lord Protector behind it, many extravagant forms of nonconformity arose.

Lollardy was not dead. It made local and popular appearances in the activities of parties like the *Diggers* and the *Levellers*. The political elements in these parties are obvious and the 'militant' wing of the British Labour Party today looks back to them with approval. They were primarily eccentric social movements. John Lilburne, who died in 1657, became the centre of the Levellers, a group who sought the dissolution of Parliament and a truly democratic rule for the country. Gerard Winstanley, in 1649, gathered around him a company of Diggers, who sought to propogate a communistic way of life. To that end, they took possession of certain Crown properties in common land and proceeded to cultivate them with their spades. Subsequent legal proceedings destroyed them. These somewhat anarchical and defiant political dissenters were paralleled on the religious side by groups like the Fifth Monarchists, who based their belief upon their reading of Daniel 2 40-44. They predicted that the present time would soon come to an end and be followed by the total reign of Christ. This had certain obvious political implications.

Religious fanaticism moved rapidly away from any connection with Wycliffe and the Lollards in a form of 'Illuminism' (doctrine of the Inner Light) called the *Ranters,* a group which denied the authority of Scripture, Christ, the Creeds and the ministry. They denied every authority whatsoever except the individual conscience. They were described by John Knox as 'Waif and stray Anabaptists looking for light'. The Quakers suffered from being associated with them in the popular mind.

Out of this period came the older Free Churches that we know today. The Quakers, always much misunderstood, had their prophet and founder in George Fox (1624-1691). He was one of the first really responsible religious leaders to accept the notion of an established and continuous Dissent. Wycliffe would have understood and sympathised with him, even if he could not understand the events of the Civil War. Erik Routley, in his *English Religious Dissent,* contrasts George Fox with other leaders of his time and, without saying as much, puts him forward as the true successor to John Wycliffe: 'It is clear that Cromwell and John Owen wanted the Church of England to be Congregational, and that the Divines wanted it Presbyterian, just as much as Laud wanted it High Church. Fox did not want the Church of England to be Quaker. He simply wanted it, in the old-fashioned sense, "pure"'. Routley also illustrates the intolerance of the Commonwealth of which Wycliffe would have strongly disapproved, and his life under Cromwell might have been no easier than under Courtenay. But Wycliffe would have approved the right to challenge authority, the decisive steps taken towards a 'good' Parliament and the firmly entrenched authority of the Bible. Without him, there would probably have been no Commonwealth, with all its faults. And, without him, that respect for the Bible as the word of God, adequate for salvation and authoritative above all human 'lords', would have grown more slowly in the land. He would without doubt have also approved Cromwell's determination to make England independent of all foreign powers in matters of church and state. None of these things could have happened without the divisions which liberty brings. Hence, English Dissent is one of Wycliffe's teaching and the practice of his Poor Preachers.

The Mother of Parliaments

The most obvious result of the success of the Parliamentarians was the securing of the authority of Parliament; but Cromwell's rough dissolving of the Long Parliament did not at the time look like that!

Parliament was established before the time of Wycliffe. A good date to assign to its birth is 1295. Thirty years earlier Simon de Montfort had, by summoning the knights and burgesses, brought a new feature into the representation of the English people, and Edward I had on various occasions asked the shires and towns for advice. But not until 1295 was the principle established: 'what touches all shall be approved by all'. A crisis in the relations of England and France forced Edward to convene the Commons for the purpose of raising a subsidy. The words of the summons include: 'We therefore firmly enjoin you to have chosen without delay and sent to us at the said day and place two knights from the said county, and two burgesses from each borough, of those more discreet and powerful to achieve! The King asks that they come 'with full and sufficient power, on behalf of themselves and the community of the counties, cities and boroughs to do what may then be ordained by the common council in the premises'. Much of the history of Parliament from that beginning was to see that the representatives had power to be more than just a rubber stamp for the king's expenses.

Parliament had not grown to its full stature in Wycliffe's day, but he treated it with respect and, when he appeared before it, he spoke with care. Wycliffe himself and his followers, the Lollards, were more than once saved by the House of Commons asserting their authority. When, in 1382, the church was in full cry and the prelates seemed to have the ear of the King, the Commons intervened. The ordinance which had been passed by the King and the Lords had put the sheriffs and state officials at the service of the church, to facilitate the arrest of unlicensed preachers. In July, Richard had sent out a special writ with orders to arrest all Lollards, as he wished to have no heresy in his kingdom. But the Commons felt otherwise. In October they insisted on the withdrawal of the ordinance of May in which they had not concurred. Their words of complaint are recorded: 'It was never assented to or granted by the Commons, but whatever was said about it has been without their consent. Let it now be annulled, for it was not the intention of the Commons, to be tried for heresy, nor to bind over themselves or their descendants to the prelates more than their ancestors had been in time past.'

That is a most significant complaint from Wycliffe's England and there is no doubt that it represents his view. England was to become accustomed to religious persecution under Tudors and Stuarts, Protestant and Catholic. Both Henry Tudor and James Stuart were Celts and it is noticeable that the Civil War was led by a true Englishman in Oliver Cromwell. Wycliffe would have recognised his kin, even if he would have disapproved strongly of many things he did. Wycliffe would no doubt have been confused by all the religious sects that arose, but in many ways his own Bible and freedom of direct access to it prepared the way for them.

The political elements are more difficult to assess. He could not approve of the execution of the King — he lived in the wrong century for that. He would, however, if true to his teaching, have approved of the trial even of a monarch, certainly of Archbishop Laud. The Commonwealth failed as a political system, but it established the House of Commons as the place of authority and it made possible the constitutional monarchy that came with William and Mary in 1688. All that was in direct line with Wycliffe's teaching.

9. Wycliffe and the Evangelical Revival

There was much in Cromwell's religion which goes back to Wycliffe. He was a man firmly rooted in the Bible and finding it his sole authority. He was a man full to the brim with the sense of God. He pursued a dream, not unlike that of Piers Plowman at Malvern – a happy England beloved of God. In his declaration of 23 May 1654, he claimed ecstatically that the place of England in the world was as if God had said: 'England thou art my first-born, my delight among the nations, under the whole heavens the Lord hath not dealt so with any of the people round about us'. Wycliffe could never have used such extravagant language, but the sentiment is in line with his patriotism and his concern for England's special place.

Like Wycliffe, Cromwell was hostile, not so much to a national church, a broad common way of worship, as to the whole apparatus of privilege and power by which the church maintained itself. Unlike Wycliffe, he saw that this apparatus was bound up with the ideology and the realities of kingship. A theory of divine monarchy implied the divinity of the church: ordinary people were not to question its rights and rules. In that last thought, Wycliffe acknowledged the latter factor, but did not equate it with the former, perhaps because the ideology of kingship had not yet been recognised.

Parliament favoured a Presbyterian settlement like that which Knox had brought to Scotland from Geneva. Cromwell did not and, with his Army, he prevented it. The Puritan revolution petered out in disputes between Independents and Presbyterians, between a rigid Calvinism, echoed in the Westminster Confession of 1643, and the warm evangelism of the independent preachers. The Restoration of the monarchy was inevitable, but Puritanism had not failed. Nothing that was really worth while in the work of Puritanism had been un-done. When we discount the dissolute courtiers and the corrupt statesmen, the mass of English people were still what Puritanism had made them, serious, earnest, sober in life and conduct, firm in their love of Protestantism and freedom. These are the sentiments of J R Green in his *A Short History of the English People,* and he concludes: 'The whole history of English progress since the Reformation, on its moral and spiritual sides, has been the history of Puritanism.'

Methodism

The Glorious Revolution of 1688 had provided a constitutional monarchy and, particularly under Queen Anne, a triumphant Church of England. It was the remnants of a Puritan and Calvinistic church, informed by rational learning and prosperous in a middle class kind of way. The old abuses of proud prelates were gone and the Anglican clergy settled down to enjoy their privileges without too much enthusiasm. On to that stage stepped the most dramatic figure of the eighteenth century – John Wesley.

Wesley rejected the Calvinism which had paralised the evangelical fervour of the Church of England, and set England ablaze with another kind of revolution. England had never before witnessed such a wave of religious fervour as that which brought 20,000 poor people together in one place to listen to one Church of England priest. There is no exact parallel with Wycliffe's England, but the poverty following upon the Black Death and subsequent inept attempts to keep wages down while prices rose, presents some elements of similarity to the eighteenth century. The period of Wesley's greatest influence was the Industrial Revolution, which created the landless poor, who were being absorbed as 'hands' in what Blake called the 'dark satanic mills'. That there was no equivalent in 1781 to the Peasants' Revolt of 1381 is in no small measure due to the influence of John Wesley. His unordained preachers were the Lollards of his century. The poor found their identity as souls deserving of salvation. When society failed them, they took hope and courage from the kingdom which transcended all societies. Thus was born what Leslie Paul describes as: 'a Christian stoicism, which distinguished the working-class of Britain in the nineteenth century and brought it uncrushed through the evils of that bad time'.

Although Methodism had its Calvinistic wing in George Whitfield, it largely rejected the doctrine of predestination which had paralysed evangelism. Warm, passionate, and confronting the hungry masses with the promise of salvation, it was not in its emotional nature to go along with a doctrine which taught the salvation of a predestined élite.

The Church of England had its own profound evangelical revival, which ran parallel with Methodism, but occasioned no further breakaway. The Evangelicals remained faithful to the Anglican Church. They were Calvinist, and saw in the Thirty Nine Articles the expression of their theology. Their revival was aimed at maintaining the purity of doctrine and practice of the Church of England.

Doctrines taught by Wycliffe

Before examining the debt of the Evangelicals to the teaching of John Wycliffe it would be well to summarise that teaching. We cannot expect, in the fourteenth century, the carefully worked out systems of 'Christian dogmatics 'which came out of the struggles of the subsequent centuries. Wycliffe was a pioneer, not a systematiser. But his teaching is clear. Wycliffe's faith was derived from the Scriptures. He regarded them as a divine revelation, containing a sufficient and perfect rule of Christian belief and practice. He considered the authority of Scripture to be superior to that of any other writing or tradition. He regarded the canonical books alone as inspired. He taught that all truth is contained in Scripture, and that no conclusion was to be allowed unless sanctioned by the sacred records. The pope's authority, or right to interfere in temporal concerns, he wholly rejected, and considered that it was only to be admitted in other respects, when conformable to Scripture.

He considered the church of Christ to be the universal congregation of those predestined to life eternal. He did not allow that the pope was head of the church, and opposed the extravagant authority claimed by the hierarchy. When this authority was asserted by the pope or, on his behalf, by the clergy at large, he did not hesitate to call it Antichrist; but nonetheless he urged respect for consistent and holy ministers of the word. He supported the king's supremacy over all persons, including clergy, in all temporal matters. Although he sometimes referred to seven sacraments, he laid stress only on two − baptism and the Lord's Supper. He rejected transubstantiation, but taught the real presence of Christ at the Lord's Supper. The bread and wine should be venerated, but not worshipped.

He approved of public worship, but condemned superstitious elements, such as the magical powers of relics and the efficacy of pilgrimages. He also disapproved of church music in worship. He admitted the doctrine of purgatory, but rejected any idea that the pains of those suffering there could be shortened by prayers offered on earth or by the intercession of the saints. For Wycliffe, purgatory was merely an intermediate state where the saints were purged of their sins. But for those who wished to assist them, he simply quoted the words of Christ, 'Let the dead bury their dead'.

He honoured the memory of the saints, but only for the example they showed to Christians that they might lead better lives here on earth. He denied the efficacy of their mediation, claiming that there is only One Mediator. He condemned the papal doctrine of indulgences in the strongest terms. He did not deny the need of the clergy to have proper provision, neither did he condemn tithes outright. He did, however, teach that when the clergy were wicked, tithes might be withheld.

Wycliffe believed in predestination and the doctrine of final perseverance: those who have received grace through Christ, cannot be finally lost. Basing his teaching as always on the Scriptures, he taught justification by faith: faith in Jesus Christ is sufficient for salvation. He persuaded people therefore to trust in Christ alone and not to seek to be justified except by his righteousness.

Wycliffe comes very close to Luther in his teaching, but he was too early to develop so systematic a doctrine. Many of his writings pass from error to truth, and it is dangerous to take a stand on one document alone. Luther was more consistent. But in one thing Wycliffe went further Luther, who never quite broke away from the transubstantiation doctrine of the Catholic Church. When eventually the teaching of Luther reached England it found the soil prepared.

For England, this morning star shone brightest as it was setting and Wycliffe's later writings are more clearly those of the coming Reformation and anticipate the Evangelical Doctrine.

Early leaders of the Evangelical Revival

The movement began in the eighteenth century and formed the religious life of England in the first half of the nineteenth. One of the early leaders was John Newton (1725-1807), who was a good example of conversion, which was always to mean so much to the Evangelicals. He ran away to sea as a boy and became the captain of a slave ship. His life was profligate until he experienced a sudden conversion in 1748. He found some difficulty in getting ordained, but eventually became vicar of Olney, and it was there that he made the acquaintance of the poet, William Cowper. John Newton and William

Cowper brought evangelical hymns into the movement, much as Isacc Watts and Charles Wesley did into Methodism.

The Evangelical Movement has been marked by song ever since. It is said of some meetings during the Welsh Revival that the crowds prevented the preacher from getting to the pulpit, but nevertheless souls were saved by the power of the singing! Wycliffe found music trivial, but he never heard a congregation sing 'O for a closer walk with God', nor 'Glorious things of thee are spoken, Zion, city of our God', nor 'How sweet the name of Jesus sounds' — all of which hymns and more came from Olney.

The later Evangelicals

Beginning in pure joy, the Evangelicals were soon involved in bitter controversy. Wycliffe had not failed to rouse fierce opposition once he attacked transubstantiation and it was on similar matters that the later Evangelicals met their bitterest attacks. This is well illustrated in the life of Charles Simeon (1759-1836).

Simeon was brought up in the High Church tradition and underwent a conversion while an undergraduate at Kings College, Cambridge. Because he was convinced that only an inner experience, a conscious sense of salvation and justification, would allow him to receive the sacrament worthily, he joined the Evangelicals. This was a deliberate rejection of the High Church party, who seemed to him to require only the outward signs of conformity. He showed such enthusiasm that it almost appeared as though he was proclaiming a new faith. When he was appointed perpetual curate at Holy Trinity in 1782 there were demonstrations against the appointment. He was a man of courage and learning, a great preacher and influential throughout the land. When he died, some over-enthusiastic supporters bought up the control of certain livings and secured them in perpetuity for Evangelicals. This illiberal action would not have earned the approval of Wycliffe, although he too would have wanted godly-men, well versed in the Scriptures, in those livings.

A careful survey of these later Evangelicals shows how closely they adhered, as their successors still do, to the Wycliffian position as it developed after the Reformation, and was preached and supported by those who insisted that the Church of England was Protestant. The High Church party prefered the official definition of 'Catholic and Reformed'.

These Evangelicals of the Revival were all aware of the power of conversion. They were Calvinists, who despite the warm and emotional mood of the beginning of the movement, began to produce a particular kind of pietist: firm – almost hard, and ready to suppress the emotions. They differed considerably from the Methodists, who were described as 'loving, yielding, even soft'. In their personal lives these Evangelicals were latter-day Puritans – sober, thrifty, hard working and earnest. This strict sense of private morals and respectability changed the face of accepted life in Victorian England. The Queen herself gave support to this view of the Church of England, and the dissolute ways of the Georgians were not condoned. In this too the Evangelicals were followers of Wycliffe. The ideal of the nineteenth century was the modest, puritan gentleman with a house and garden in the suburbs, and the high esteem of his church or chapel. To this ideal, the lower middle classes almost universally aspired. It was called 'respectability' and carried no derisory ring, such as the word acquired later. It meant then simply, 'being worthy of respect'.

The Evangelicals were never nearer to Wycliffe's ideal than when they ceased to respect that hierarchical pattern of pope (or archbishop) at the top, graded spiritually down to the laypeople. Like the Wycliffe who could say that a pauper who was virtuous had more right to lordship than a wicked pope, they democratised spirituality. Wesley had done the same. The personal experience of conversion or salvation, the motion of God directly into the heart of the Christian, the inner proof of election — such were independent of hierarchical status and cultural privileges.

The Evangelicals also crossed denominational boundaries, which Wycliffe could not have understood, because there was only one denomination in England in his day. But the Lollards would most certainly have done the same as the Evangelicals if they had encountered fellow-Christians of like faith. Loyal as the Evangelicals were to the Church of England as by Parliament established, they were even more bitterly opposed to the High Church party in their own church than they were to Rome. They can be said to have persecuted the Anglo-Catholics as illegal and subversive throughout the nineteenth century. Their true spiritual kin were the evangelicals — Calvinist and fundamentalist — of the other denominations. This took institutional form in the Evangelical Alliance which was formed in 1846, drawing 900 clergy and laity from all over the world. It was an international, ecumenical assertion of their common position. Thus united, the Evangelical conscience (indistinguishable from the Non-conformist conscience) had an unparalleled effect upon the politics of the century.

10. English Nonconformity and its debt to Wycliffe

In the last chapter of his book *English Religious Dissent,* Erik Routley poses the question about the need for 'Dissent'. In order to answer it he has to show, that Dissent goes back well before 1662. Although today Dissent in the form of grievance is dead, there are things against which Dissenters have always stood and these are more fundamental, he maintains, than their grievances which are merely temporary symptons of the wrongs against which they protest. These fundamental wrongs he defines as 'obscurantism and spiritual tyranny'. These are not temporary. In many ways they are at the heart of Wycliffe's Dissent.

The obscurantism of the medieval church, which left ordinary people wondering and helpless before its contrived miracles, angered Wycliffe as he probed into its untruth. His bitterest attacks on the friars was for their fooling of the people and preaching an obscure gospel that left bewildered hearers at the mercy of these clever merchants of spiritual things. For this reason he insisted upon a vernacular Bible and direct access for all to the word of God or, as he would say, 'Goddis lawe'. As his opponents saw, this would inevitably lead to differences of interpretation and end the absolute authority of the priest.

The same applies to his attack upon transubstantiation. The spiritual tyranny of the priest dispensing Christ's body, needful for salvation, was paramount. Wycliffe gradually moved the validity of the sacrament away from the priest to the congregation of the faithful. Again, his teaching on lordship undermined the rights of the prelate to lordship, as it did those of the immoral lord.

If Erik Routley is right in saying that what the Dissenters stood for was an opposition to obscurantism and spiritual tyranny, then Wycliffe is their first leader.

Of course, not all Dissenters left the Church of England. To this day, the most powerful opponents of obscurantism and spiritual tyranny will be found in the Church of England itself and it has always been so. Wycliffe remained within the church of his day. But England has developed a structure of Nonconformity which is unparalleled in any other European country and it has been the main element in the structure of American religious life.

The origins of Nonconformity

The inter-dependence of Anabaptists and Lollards, the influence of Luther and Calvin disseminated by the invention of printing, the heady draft of the Renaissance, all have their part in providing the soil for English Nonconformity. But the early English Dissenters did not preach Luther or Calvin. They preached the gospel. They gathered congregations and preached it believing that it justified the legitimate claims of the under-privileged. It was not a gospel of peace, but of controversy, and it was not very consistent. They lived in an age of controversy and inconsistency! But they were human beings living in an age where, for the historian looking back, it is very hard to decide who was right.

In the sixteenth century, when Henry made his break with Rome, there were many different opinions about the nature of the emerging English Church. Wycliffe would no doubt have supported Henry, and in fact he had already drafted the kind of constitution the Church of England ultimately adopted. The king at the head, with the bishops and clergy deriving authority from him, was Wycliffe's model. Whether he would have held it still in the sixteenth century it is hard to say. Those who opposed the church/state settlement were often closer to Wycliffe in other matters than were the supporters of Henry's church. The issue was the importance to be attached to church and state. If you believed that church and state were two authorities which must cross-fertilise each other, both ordained by God for the same ultimate purpose — as Wycliffe did and Luther after him — then Henry's solution was right. It seemed to most people that the appointment of bishops by the Crown was a good thing, but there were some who did not trust the Crown or the time-servers who advised Henry. Nonetheless, he carried the majority of the population with him because of the general dislike of Rome.

What followed was not encouraging. After Henry's death, the young King was manipulated by advisers and then, in reaction to an extreme form of Protestantism, Mary was able to impose the old Catholic faith by force and violence. After Mary, there were many who saw that Henry's solution would not do. Those who tried to change things under Elizabeth were divided into reformers and revolutionaries — i.e. Anglican Puritans and 'Separatist' Puritans.

The primacy of Scripture

One of Wycliffe's battles had been won, and on this both reformers and revolutionaries agreed. It was now assumed in England that all Christians were mature enough to read their own Bibles. All Puritans insisted that the Scriptures were the only authority for guidance in the matter of church order and Christian behaviour. But how were they to understand the Bible? Should Scripture be literally interpreted, Scripture's silence taken as prohibition, all that it says taken as unquestioned commands? The early Puritans were scholars and understood their Bible, but many who read their vernacular Bible had no means by which to unlock its meaning, no sense of the different types of literature it contained and the different ways of using different parts. They were slow to recognise that the proper handling of the Bible involves the willingness and ability to distinguish between one kind of literature and another. For this reason it soon became plain that the vernacular Bible was to be a source not of reconciliation but of conflict.

The first Separatists

In 1567, a minister and some of his congregation of about 100 people were arrested and called upon to explain their 'Separatist' meeting. They objected to the wearing of surplices and copes in church and to the presumed authority of the sovereign to insist upon this. There is a Lollard-like simplicity in their protests – both the trivial matter of the surplices and the more fundamental issue of whether the sovereign has a right to dictate how God should be worshipped. Wycliffe saw the king as an acceptable authority to control the proud prelates and would vest the rights of property in him, for the sake of the nation. He saw the seizing of church property as lawful, but properly used to relieve the poverty of the poor. He did not approve of the king, or any man or woman, dictating how God should be worshipped, unless it could be demonstrated that the command came from Scripture.

In documents describing other congregations about this time we can detect many Lollard-like tendencies. One from 1571 was signed by twenty seven members of a Separatist congregation:

> 'We are a poor congregation whom God has
> separated from the Church of England, and
> from the mingled and false worshipping therin,
> out of the which assemblies the Lord our only
> Saviour hath called us, and still calleth, saying,
> ''Come out from among them, and separate
> yourselves from them, and touch no unclean
> thing, then will I receive you, and I will be
> your God'.'

RW Dale in his *History of English Congregationalism* quotes another document of the period which contains the same Lollard-like humility and striving for holiness.

It also insists upon the 'purity' of preaching, which means on the authority of Scripture alone. If the interpretation is literal and rationalistic, it must be remembered that these Separatists, like the Lollards, were defending the Scriptures against elaborate misinterpretations. There was a patriotic sense also in this congregation, which echoed Wycliffe. They insisted upon separation for the nation's sake, from Romish and heathen practices. The document quoted by Dale introduces a contrast between the Anglicans who are described as obedient to canon law ('filthy canon law') as a test of their churchmanship, and that 'gospel freedom' which they intended to be the mark of their new church. This church, led by one Richard Fitz, went underground.

Robert Browne

Leaving aside the shadowy figure of Richard Fitz, whose underground church disappears from history, the pioneer of English Nonconformity was the stormy Robert Browne. Born about 1550, he is first heard of when, as an Anglican cleric, he refers to the settled ministry as a 'bondage'. When invited to preach at a church in Cambridge, he strongly insisted that this preaching was not a settled ministry. 'Whoever would take charge of them (the congregation)', he says, 'must also come into bondage with them'.

In 1579, Browne was preaching against the calling and authorisation of preachers by bishops. He seeks instead Wycliffe's freedom to send out preachers without reference to the bishops! It was not long before he was inhibited from preaching, by an order of the bishop, delivered and read to him by a future Archbishop of Canterbury (Richard Bancroft, at that time Bishop's Chancellor). He left Cambridge and turned to school teaching. In Norwich, where he taught, he was soon in trouble. In 1580 a complaint was made that certain 'lewde Scholemasters' were corrupting the minds of the children in East Anglia. While in Norwich he came to the conclusion that the only way for true Reformation was to separate from the Church of England. He left Norwich and went to London where he was imprisoned for Nonconformity.

Robert Browne soon had a following and his 'Brownists' were not unlike latter-day Lollards. But they found that England was no place for them. Some decided to go to Scotland where John Knox's Reformation was well entrenched, but Browne chose to go to Holland. He was invited to Middelburg where certain Dutch merchants who had visited Norwich were sympathetic to his preaching. He joined a fellow English Puritan, Cartwright, who had a congregation there, but soon formed one of his own. He wrote his three famous books there: *A Treatise of Reformation without Tarrying for Anie, A Treatise upon the 23 of Matthew,* and *A Book that sheweth the Life and Manners of all True Christians.* But he was uneasy. 'Instead of one pope there', he commented, 'I found a thousand!'. He returned to England.

In 1585, he was charged before Archbishop Whitgift for a book he had written, against Cartwright, of all people. He signed a recantation and was appointed master of St Olave's School in Southwark. His protector was Lord Burghley, a distant relative. Despite frequently preaching in Dissenting conventicles he kept out of trouble, largely due to Burghley's protection. In 1591, he conformed and became first deacon, then priest of the Church of England. In many ways he remained a Dissenter, preaching in a Dissenting conventicle for ten years, during which time he was suspended. However, in 1631, he was appointed rector of a church in Northamptonshire. But by 1632, when he was well beyond the age of eighty, he was imprisoned for the thirty second and last time. He died in October 1633.

I have told his story in some detail, because of his importance for the understanding of Nonconformity before the Civil War, and the even greater importance of the

Brownists, whose activities link Wycliffe with the revolutionary Reformation which was an inevitable part of Puritanism. We can feel some sympathy with those who had to deal with Robert Browne. He was difficult and inconsistent, but he never allowed himself to be diverted from one positive proposition, and it is vital to English Nonconformity: 'only proved Christians can constitute a church'. Christians alone! That is where the controversy of historic English Dissent always begins. Holiness is inseparable from the gathered and covenanted church, and Christians must be separated uncompromisingly from the world.

That begs all kinds of questions about how to decide who is a true Christian. For Robert Browne and for those who followed him it is impossible to conceive of a true church constituted legalistically. In his *Life and Manners,* he attacked all popish churches and he virtually includes the Church of England, whom he strongly contrasted with that 'Communion of Graces' which he deemed to be the true church.

The Congregationalists are the descendants of Robert Browne, even though they may not support all his statements. In these days, some of them have gone to Scotland, or at least joined with the English Presbyterians in the United Reformed Church, but a vigorous remnant continues in the ways of Robert Browne as the Congregational Federation, while others have recognised their home as being with those of the Evangelical Revival.

The Baptists

A contemporary of Robert Browne was John Smyth (1565 – 1612). He was successively a Puritan, a Separatist, a Baptist and an Anabaptist. Different scholars have tried to find a consistent doctrine in John Smyth and have variously suggested, with documentary evidence, that he maintained the idea of the covenant through his various changes, and that he never wavered from the crucial doctrine of 'the resurrected' Christ in His character as Ruling King'.

He also began in Cambridge and, as a Puritan, he was orthodox and firm, abhorring toleration, insisting that magistrates should compel all people to worship the true God. The only trace of heresy in this Puritan period, which lasted until 1605, was that he urged that magistrates should not persecute the true church, nor be followed when they acted contrary to God's word. One can recognise Wycliffe's views here.

Smyth became a Separatist around 1605. He remained a Calvinist and opposed the Anabaptists. During the next few years his attention was directed to the doctrine of the church. He maintained that Puritans agreed with the Separatists in all but separation, and then proceeded to show that the idea of separation derives from Calvin's *Institutes*. He attempted to show that the Church of England was potentially a false church and for that reason the true Christians must separate from it.

But it was in 1609 that John Smyth made his drastic change. He rejected infant baptism and rebaptised himself and his followers. Much of his earlier writing might have led us to believe that he was just rejecting Anglican baptism, but this was more than that. He now totally rejected infant baptism and instituted believers' baptism. From this beginning came the General Baptists. Despite the rebaptism, John Smyth continued to be an orthodox Puritan and Calvinistic Separatist. But he was already tending away from his earlier detailed interpretation of the covenant. In fact, believers' baptism was becoming a substitute for the covenant. He separated now both from the Anglicans and from the Separatists. His new definition of the true church as constituted by believers' baptism led him to the Anabaptists.

In February 1610 Smyth and many of his followers applied to join the Waterlander Mennonite Church in Holland. Thomas Helwys was to learn believers' baptism from these brethren in Holland and return to England to give the Baptists another founder. His *Mystery of Iniquity*, for which he was imprisoned, was very close at several points to the teaching of Wycliffe, particularly in the limitations which he puts upon lordship.

The growing company of Nonconformists

The Civil War, as we have seen, brought many splinter movements into the Puritan camp. All the older 'Free Churches' (a name that was not used until 1895) saw their first period of growth under Cromwell. The second period was the year 1662, when so many Puritans among the Anglicans resisted the Act of Uniformity. The eighteenth century saw the rise of Methodism, which never intended to be Separatist. To his death, John Wesley regarded himself as a priest of the Church of England.

The nineteenth century saw the growth of Nonconformity until it almost dominated the religious life of the country. The support which Evangelicals gave to the formation of Bible societies and missionary societies of all denominations showed them to be the natural allies of the Nonconformists. It was in the nineteenth century that Wycliffe was rediscovered and used as a weapon against the 'High Church movement' within the Church of England, which both Anglican Evangelicals and Nonconformists resisted. They saw in the Oxford Movement an attempt to bring back Roman domination.

The story of the Ecumenical Movement does not belong to this volume, but it is an indication, as is the growth of the Evangelical Alliance, that the twentieth century is getting nearer to Wycliffe, for whom there was one church in England, with all its disputes and differences within that church. One suspects that John Wycliffe would feel himself very much at home in a 'World Conference on Faith and Order', although he would be very wary of the Roman Catholic observers and very surprised when some of them supported his views!

11. The importance of Wycliffe today

Our own attitude to Wycliffe might well be that of his attitude to the saints. They are not to be mediators between God and man, they are not to be worshipped, but they may be honoured for the example they give to us for our Christian way of life. Wycliffe's writings are of the fourteenth century and sound strange in our ears. Even his translation of the Bible will not do for a generation that has behind it so much herioc and accurate scholarship, and far better translation than his.

But as we honour him for what he did in his generation, we are aware that he made certain permanent contributions which are of essential value to us today.

The Bible

Wycliffe set in motion a process which issued in Tyndale, the Authorised Version, the Revised Standard Version, J B Phillips, the Good News Bible, the New International Version. He is the grandfather of the Bible societies which have served the churches in every land and every denomination.

We shall learn little by reading his comments today, because he communicated to his own generation; but he left an attitude to the Bible that has remained the predominant English (and later American) position ever since. It can be summed up in the word 'confidence'. Through the blizzard of critical scholarship in the nineteenth century and the arid debate between fundamentalists and modernists in the twentieth, the British retained a confidence in the Bible which kept their heads above water. A German scholar coming to Oxford expressed this quite simply by saying that in Germany you tried to find out where the Bible was wrong; in England you assumed it was true, and then tried to handle the difficulties created by mistakes you discovered in it. This we owe to Wycliffe. We have travelled a long way since his literal acceptance of the text of Scripture, but our discussions concern details – the date and authorship of certain books, the exact text, the deeper meaning when a text is expressed in primitive ideas etc. We retain a belief in the Bible as an incomparable authority and are convinced that if we work at it, trying honestly to understand, God will mediate his will to us through it in a way that we do not find in any other writing.

We trust the Bible more than we trust the Creeds or the decisions of councils. It is also to Wycliffe that we owe the clear distinction between the canon of Old and New Testament on the one hand and apocryphal books on the other. We read the Books of the Maccabees as we read Josophus; neither are the Bible. After all the centuries of critical study we retain a respect for the authority of the Bible and a confidence in its message.

The Responsibilities of power

Wycliffe never allowed the proud prelate or the secular lord to forget that 'lordship' was held by permission of God, and account must be made to him for it. Only those 'in grace' can lawfully hold authority in church or state. As soon as they begin to think that they have power by right, and can use it as they please, they become illegitimate.

This teaching in different forms, and challenged at certain periods of our history, has never disappeared. The bishop knew that in England, at least, unless he exercised his power rightly and lived a life which matched his profession, he would not be respected or obeyed. Even the mill owner knew that his 'hands' would not respect or obey him if they were convinced that he was unjust. The democratisation of the bishop in the church and the rise of trade unions are twin shoots from the teaching of Wycliffe. He condemned neither episcopacy nor hereditary wealth, but he required both to be justified before God and the people.

While Wycliffe respected both king and Parliament he did not cease to remind them that their authority was under the word of God. Even the pope, or perhaps, *especially* the pope, had to show that his actions were in conformity with the word of God. That was more than simply a statement about the superior authority of the Bible. It was a basic teaching which has persisted through our history and is not forgotten today. No one who holds power – not even the elected representative of the people, by whatever size the majority – is above scrutiny.

The revolutionary nature of this teaching about the conditions of power, and the responsibilities of those who hold it, is not always recognised. Today, it challenges the rights of parliaments, judges, police, priests, governments in power. None of these have a mandate which cannot be challenged by reason or tested by a commonly accepted morality. In our complex, pluralistic society, it is sometimes difficult to know what is right or wrong, even to understand what is being done. But in a country which has inherited the courage of John Wycliffe, the efforts to understand must be made and no power must be allowed to go unchallenged.

The greatest problem today probably comes from the media, whose experts can manipulate the mind of the masses. Wycliffe would, like Milton after him, allow their freedom and rejoice at much of the best investigative journalism, but he would also require them to be accountable.

In one of his many bitter attacks upon the friars selling indulgences, Wycliffe shows his attitude to the secular power and he demands the same controls for religious power over lay people: 'Do not these deceivers know that men who have the disposal of temporal goods have their superiors and known laws, to which they are responsible, while the dealers in these supposed "merits of men" dispense their wares "after their own will?"'

The rights of all

We have constantly to remember that Wycliffe lived in the fourteenth century and that, just as Paul did not directly attack the slavery of his day, Wycliffe accepted the social order. Within that social order he had much to say about the rights of all. In fact, Paul's letters – and Peter's – gave him a pattern for his treatise on *Servants and Masters*. He repudiated the facile arguments of his day, often heard before and during the Peasants' Revolt, that no Christians should be servants because they could not serve a heathen lord and a Christian lord was their equal. Instead, Wycliffe goes to great lengths – twenty five pages – to show 'that servants should truly and gladly serve their lords and masters, and not be false or idle, nor grudging.' But he gives equal length to the behaviour of lords in respecting the rights of their servants.

If the people owe obedience to lords, lords owe justice, protection and kind offices to those below them. They should 'know God's law and study it and maintain it', living godly and peaceful lives and protecting the rights of the poor to do likewise. He does not leave these as vague general rights, but spells them out. Others have written more precisely about human rights, but here, already in the fourteenth century, is one who lays down the foundations, not in any partisan way, but on the basis of biblical study. He does not plead for compassion, but asserts the right of God to demand this of people, on pain of losing their lordship.

This approach to social ethics is of continuing importance today. Wycliffe found a land under tutelage to the church, which had the power to preserve the people's rights and the privileges of others. He saw the rights whittled away through greed, and the privileges unjustly maintained by clerical authority. He changed the basis of justice from dependence upon the righteous church to natural and biblical authority. So that the church could be challenged as well as the secular lords.

Rights are not granted by acts of Parliament or decrees from church or state authorities. There exist natural, inalienable rights for all people. We still need that emphasis.

One church, one nation

Wycliffe lived before the times of Separatist denominations and never faced the ecumenical question in the way that we face it. But he had much to say about the unity and the autonomy of the nation and the church. The divisions in his day were between privilege and poverty, between a papal church and an English church. What he says about the political situation of a divided land is of continuing importance. We hear from him no superficial call for unity, much as he desired that. His theological interpretation of political power as being always under God, led him to demand equal spiritual rights for all. The Bible should be available to all. No one should hold another in thrall because he has spiritual superiority, either of understanding or sacramental rights.

Wycliffe understood the demands of peasants for their rights. He pleaded for them after the Revolt failed. He could not tolerate a wealthy church in a poor land, nor an arrogant priest withholding religious rights. His message to both lord and servant was that they had a common enemy in the counterfeit powers of church and state. His most unbridled venom was reserved for those who pretended to spiritual superiority and used their privileges to fool the poor with phoney religion.

He realised that this was possible because of the lack of discipline in the religious orders, and attacked any pretence in a friar or monk of being a superior Christian to a ploughman. He saw in the unaccountable authority of the religious orders a threat to the unity of the country as well as to the church in England.

It was this above all which called forth his bitter attacks upon the pope. The right of the pope to have his battalions of priests in England divided the country. King and pope may make a compromise, but the division of their spoils led to the division of the land and people. It was this that made the attack on the rights of sanctuary so serious. Wycliffe did not approve of killing a man at the altar, but he would not tolerate two laws in the land — one for the church and another for the people, one for the rich and another for the poor. This was another trail he blazed and it has not finished burning yet. It was part of his passion for one nation.

Although Wycliffe lived before the denominations, he did not live before the orders, and he treated them as dangerous to the unity of church and state. Before the King and Parliament he maintained boldly: 'Christ's rule is enough, and able for all men whatever complexion they be or whatever age. This rule was kept of Jesus Christ and of his apostles and the best of their followers for five hundred years after the ascension, without any finding of any such new planting, or religion, in which Holy church increased and profited much'. He speaks out strongly against the rule of friars and urges the pope to: 'dispense with the rule of each private sect or religion'.

The absolute essential for all Christians is 'Christ's rule given to the apostles', and all else simply divides. Wycliffe's advice to Parliament quoted above would appear to put him among the ecumenically minded of our day, but before we attempt to classify him we must remember that he is talking about the basis of the one church being built upon the Gospels — and nothing else.

Reason and the individual

Wycliffe gave to England a good commonsense attitude to religion. In any dispute he would appeal to the plain sense of reason, when he was not quoting from the Bible. And he clearly believed that the Bible was not a mysterious book. He has bequeathed to us an attitude to the Bible as meeting this plain sense of reason, which has stood us in good stead throughout the centuries and stands still.

When a group meets for Bible study it is all too easy to become esoteric. The Middle Ages gave such fanciful meanings to the Scriptures that only the priests who were thought to be in the know could interpret. For that reason they thought there was little point in putting the Bible into English, for the ordinary people would not understand it. Wycliffe opposed that strongly. He believed that the simplest men or women could understand the Bible in their own language.

Nothing angered him more than the fanciful stories the friars told — more about the Trojan War than the Bible! These classical stories were often blended with biblical stories to amuse the people. The friars thus became popular story-tellers and they opposed the provision of a Bible that the layperson could read and understand.

We have got back to Wycliffe's attitude. The old allegorical interpretation has slowly gone. Even Latimer could interpret the parable of the Good Samaritan in an esoteric way, making the two pence that was given to the innkeeper a symbol of the two natures in Christ. Wycliffe was capable of doing this with the Old Testament, but not with the Gospels. A story from the Gospels or a saying of Jesus must mean precisely what it says.

Many of Wycliffe's arguments against transubstantiation were an appeal to plain reason. The adoration of a piece of bread in the place of the Deity, Wycliffe denounced as idolatry. And conduct of the officiating priest, in pretending to remake his maker, he proclaimed as the ultimate in presumption and blasphemy.

At every point, he urged that individual Christians should use their reason, listen to the word of Scripture and open their minds to understand. This gave them direct access to the fountain of their faith. Such attitudes led to a growing concept of the responsible individual. And although Protestants have often been accused of 'individualism' it is the glory of Wycliffe that he taught the dignity of the Christian individual, who has the ability to stand before God without any other Mediator than Christ, to hear and bear the word of God without benefit of clergy and to recognise his or her worth as a forgiven child of God.

John Wycliffe

In Balliol College, Oxford, where he spent most of his active life, there hangs a portrait of John Wycliffe. He is a bearded and apparently aged man. His face is determined and his eyes seriously intent. In his gloved left hand he holds a staff, and in his right a book or file of papers. It is a good portrait of a man who has obviously suffered and is accustomed to study. There is a purpose burning in his eyes which will not be stilled. He is recognisable as the man we have been discussing in this book. For quite apart from what he did and the message he proclaimed, he was a man whom no one dared to impugn. He was upright, unafraid, persistent in the service of his Lord, a man who feared God and after that had no one else to fear.

The memory of such a man, which his contemporaries tried to erase from the nation's mind, has stiffened the resolve of this country in many times of distress. And we live in such a time. His memory and his example should enable us to face better the challenges of the eighties and nineties.

Ours are not the problems that Wycliffe faced, but his total trust in the message of the Bible as clearly applying to his day and to any day, his firm determination that every person should have direct access to the fountain of faith, his impatience with all kinds of cant, pretence, hypocrisy and unmerited privilege, his honesty and integrity, are qualities we shall need. He would not have wanted to be canonised, but he was the kind of saint he looked for and we need.

Notes

CHAPTER 1

1. G M Trevelyan *England in the Age of Wycliffe* p. 185
2. Higden *Polychronicon* (Trans. John Trevisa)

CHAPTER 2

1. Wycliffe *On Divine Lordship*
2. G M Trevelyan op. cit. p. 44-45

CHAPTER 3

1. G M Trevelyan op. cit.
2. Wycliffe, from F D Matthew *Wycliffe's English Works* p. 233-4

CHAPTER 6

1. John Huss *On Simony*

Bibliography

G.M. Trevelyan *England in the Age of Wycliffe.*

Chaucer *The Canterbury Tales.*

William Langland *Piers Plowman.*

SCM Library of Christian Classics Vols. XIV and XXV.

J.H. Merle d'Aubigné *The Reformation in England.*

Erik Routley *English Religious Dissent.*

Leslie Paul *A Church by Daylight.*

Horton Davies *The English Free Churches.*

J.R. Green *A Short History of the English People.*

R.W. Dale *History of English Congregationalism.*

Robert Vaughan *Tracts and Treatises of John de Wycliffe.*

G.W.H. Lampe *The Cambridge History of the Bible,* Vol. 2